EFFECTIVENESS
BY
THE
NUMBERS

More Praise for *Effectiveness by the Numbers*

"Feedback is the breakfast of champions. Bill Hoyt shows how to get constructive feedback on what's happening in your church—then use that information to improve. His pastor-tested and church-approved insights will help your ministry."
—Kevin Miller, Vice President, *Christianity Today International*

"*Effectiveness by the Numbers* avoids pitfalls of reductionism on the one hand (church is only what can be counted) and refusal to be accountable on the other (our church is above crassly counting numbers)....The wisdom of 'counting the right things' enables pastors and boards to analyze and understand 'what is' and then to identify pointers for decisive leadership on pathways of hope. Bill Hoyt juxtaposes biblical truth and the challenges facing contemporary churches with compelling insight about what healthy and vibrant churches look like."
—Leland Eliason, Executive Director and Provost, Bethel Seminary of Bethel University, St. Paul, Minnesota

EFFECTIVENESS BY THE NUMBERS

COUNTING WHAT *COUNTS* IN THE CHURCH

WILLIAM R. HOYT

Abingdon Press / Nashville

EFFECTIVENESS BY THE NUMBERS:
COUNTING WHAT COUNTS IN THE CHURCH

Copyright © 2007 by William R. Hoyt

All rights reserved.

This book is printed on acid-free paper.

Library of Congress Cataloging-in-Publication Data

Hoyt, William R.
  Effectiveness by the numbers: counting what counts in the church / William R. Hoyt.
    p. cm.
  ISBN-13: 978-0-687-64175-8 (pbk.: alk. paper)
  1. Church management.   2. Church statistics I. Title.
  BV652.H69 2007
  254—dc22

2007013538

07 08 09 10 11 12 13 14 15 16 —10 9 8 7 6 5 4 3 2 1

MANUFACTURED IN THE UNITED STATES OF AMERICA

I dedicate this work to my Lord, to His Church, and to my family.

These three give my life abundant meaning and joy.

CONTENTS

CD-ROM Worksheets
    Metrics Manual
    Conversions Worksheet
    Worship Attendance Worksheet
    Market Share Worksheet
    Worship Frequency Worksheet
    Visitor Retention Worksheet
    Ministry Involvement–Church Worksheet
    Ministry Involvement–Community Worksheet
    Ministry Involvement–World Worksheet
    Ministry Involvement–Composite Worksheet
    Leadership Development Worksheet
    Small Group Participation Worksheet
    Tithing–Self Identified Worksheet
    Tithing–Whole Church Worksheet

FOREWORD

Your mission is what you measure. This simple principle is what lies at the root of this book, but it is also what lies at the root of apostolic mission, earliest church experience, and Jesus' own words like "where your treasure is, there will your heart be also" (Luke 12:34). If seekers really want to know the true, authentic, constantly practiced, bottom line, "to die for," essential mission of a church ... they have only to watch what that church *measures* to determine success.

In my own experience as a pastor, denominational leader, and consultant (a similar path to friend Bill Hoyt), I have constantly observed the unwillingness of churches to measure results. This is a relatively new phenomenon in church history, having originated mid-twentieth century after the world wars, and blossomed among baby boomers for whom religion is personal, vague, and generally less important than affluence. North Americans are "results driven" in almost everything *except* religion. While we may boast that this is because religion is so important that it is beyond counting numbers, it is really because it is so unimportant that counting numbers is embarrassing or a waste of time. The post-war, boomer propaganda that churches are all about something so vast and mysterious as to be belittled by too much quantitative analysis has little to do with the history of the church or the gospel message. Ancient and non-North American churches are united in believing that Jesus wants us to be clearly accountable for getting results.

The irony is that despite our great reservations about "measuring results" in the church, we do it all the time. We just don't admit it. We camouflage our real mission (the one we actually measure), with our supposed mission (the one we publicly claim). Our mission statements are typically grounded on good intentions. We always "strive for," "desire to," and "follow faithfully," so that the only mark of success is how sincere we think we are, which is, at best, a matter of perspective. And we are always striving for "transformation," "relevance," and "inclusiveness," even though we never actually measure who or what got transformed last year, how many microcultures really connected with the church last month, or whether the world really is any different because our church existed last week. Meanwhile, beneath the public claim, *there is the reality of what we actually measure.*

What most established churches actually measure are harmony, stability, and privilege. This is what occupies the agendas of most board meetings, congregational gatherings, and denominational oversight processes.

Churches go to great lengths to measure harmony. They mark every single, conceivable, and even half-baked complaint, anxiety, or hurt feeling. They painstakingly research the grievances of members. They even know within about ninety seconds whether a worship service is too short or too long. If there were a handheld, electronic gadget that could measure the pressure of a hug during the passing of the peace, they would buy it.

Churches go to great lengths to measure stability. They chart the financial and membership trends. They have mastered the art of risk management. They know precisely how many people, in every age group, participate how many times a year in gender- and age-based groups. They know instantly the number of envelope users and families who have preauthorized their financial contributions. They are keenly aware of the minimum resources required to maintain the five supposedly essential programs of church life (namely, traditional worship, pastoral salaries, congregational fellowship, nursery, and under-eighteen ministries).

Churches go to great lengths to measure privilege. They maintain elaborate by-laws and exacting processes for consensus management. They know exactly how many board members are required to approve an idea, how many weeks are required to call a congregational meeting, and how many votes are required to set policy. They have a pretty good estimate of the top ten families that need to be consulted for every decision and how many degrees of divergence might be tolerated from aesthetic tastes and ideological opinions of the best givers.

The problem, which I describe in my recent book *Why Should I Believe You?* (also by Abingdon Press), is that seekers see, all too clearly, the disconnection between the public mission that is somehow beyond quantitative measurement, and the real mission that strains every gnat, weighs every dollar, and evaluates every minute of staff deployment.

This is why Bill Hoyt's book *Effectiveness by the Numbers* is so refreshing. Once faithful church leaders get it into their heads that the church is so vastly important that it *must* be evaluated quantitatively, they naturally wonder what to measure. What counts for success in the eyes of God? And what doesn't count as success in the eyes of God? If Jesus, the Great Steward of God's Mission, has given each church ten ingots of spiritual gold, and commanded them to go and invest wisely in order to make ten spiritual ingots more, then *what exactly would that spiritual net gain look like?* In this book, Bill tells you.

Mission is what you measure. Leaders measure what is really important, and don't bother measuring what is, in reality, unimportant. What if your heart *isn't* invested in harmony, stability, and privilege? What if your heart *is really invested* in pursuing God's mission to redeem the world, implementing Christ's strategic plan to multiply disciples one microculture at a time, and (as Paul said in 1 Corinthians 9:22) figuring out how to become all things to all people, so that by all means, the church can rescue some? The public will see it clearly. If that is what you measure, then, in heaven's name that must really be your mission!

Your next step after finishing this book will be to ponder deeply the parable of the Talents (Matthew 25:14-30). Bill refers to this passage directly in chapters 1 and 8, but they lie behind the entire book. I think we will be able to divide the readers who complete this book into three categories. Unfortunately, there will always be the unproductive servants who simply refuse to measure mission. More importantly, there will be other moderately productive servants who will learn what to measure and how to do it, and will become far more productive in the future. Finally, there are those highly productive servants who will be challenged to go farther, and risk more, than they ever dared. Having met their goals, they will realize that their goals were not high enough. When Christ is involved, the sky is the limit.

—Thomas G. Bandy
(Author of *Mission Mover*, *Roadrunner*, and *Why Should I Believe You?* . . . all from Abingdon Press)

ACKNOWLEDGMENTS

My theology of God and my philosophy of life cause me to believe that I am who I am today because of all the people and experiences God has used to mold me and shape me. God is not a God of happenstance. He is not sloppy in His dealings with us. No relationship, no encounter, no idea, no experience, no struggle, no achievement, no joy, no tear is wasted by God. He is the Master Potter, and I am grateful for His shaping of my life. Anything good, any wisdom, any insight I might have to offer is a work of His hand. The honor for anything you might gain from this book belongs to Him. It is His because without His shaping me I would have nothing of value to offer.

The list of people God has used in my life is long, and to be honest, I have forgotten most of them. In times of reflection, many come to mind, and I am grateful for every one. The impact of a few has been so penetrating they bear special mention.

- My parents, Edith and John Hoyt, who, as first-generation Christians, successfully led each of their seven children to faith in Jesus.
- My pastor Bob Paulson, whose words, "Remember, Bill, we need guys like you in the ministry," were used by God to call me to pastoral service and a life-long love affair with the church.
- Rick Sturm, a friend and fellow traveler in ministry, whose profound wisdom, unwavering integrity, and fearless leadership repeatedly humbled, instructed, and inspired me.
- Avery Powers, another friend and fellow traveler, who, in his life and his death, taught me this central Truth, "It's all about Jesus, Bill, it's ALL about JESUS!"

- Frank Green, whose ability to look deep into my inner being and speak truth has had far more impact on me than my "cherry self-image" cares to admit.
- Dennis Baker, whose involvement in my life has been profound. Our passion for God and His church is the same, but Dennis sees a world that I cannot until he shares it with me.
- Paul Borden, friend, kindred spirit, and partner in ministry without whose encouragement this book would never have been written.
- My wife, Gwyn, whose passion for Christlikeness has sanded away many of my rough edges and burrs. The remaining outcroppings of my natural temperament are not due to her failure but mine. Thankfully, neither she nor God is done with me yet!

Acknowledgment is also due the people—especially the leaders—of all the churches God has allowed me to serve. Chief among them would be the Big Springs Baptist Church (Alcester, South Dakota), Spring Lake Park Baptist Church (Spring Lake Park, Minnesota), and Lincoln Avenue Baptist Church (Escondido, California) where I was privileged to serve as Senior Pastor. And finally, thanks to the many hundreds of churches that have allowed me to observe them and participate with them in ministry as a consultant, first with the Southwest District of the Baptist General Conference and now through NexStep Coaching and Consulting. I have learned from you all. You have been God's hands shaping me for His service and yours.
—William Hoyt

INTRODUCTION

Statistics always tell a story. The doctor draws blood, the lab analyzes it, and sends a report back to the doctor. The doctor reads the numbers and can make educated guesses about your past. The numbers give him or her a clear picture of your current health status. And the numbers also predict the future unless changes are made.

The doctor says, "You've got to stop eating fatty foods, get more exercise, and reduce your cholesterol or you will have a heart attack before you're sixty." How did your physician know you eat fast food hamburgers, French fries, and milkshakes nearly every day? How did he or she know you consider a fast trip to the refrigerator during a commercial to be a serious workout? After all you are not overweight. When people ask you how you can eat as you do, you tell them you have great metabolism. Your waistline did not tell the doctor, so how did he or she know? The numbers told the story. The numbers predict a likely future unless changes are made.

In medicine, business, sports, finance, school, science, real estate, transportation, law enforcement, and construction, numbers matter. In just about every arena of life we count, keep track, and make adjustments based on statistics.

Too often the church is the notable exception. Some churches do not count. Some count sporadically, others inaccurately. Still others count a lot of things that do not really matter. In fact in some church circles people are proud of not counting. They say, "Numbers aren't everything." Their favorite is, "You can't measure spirituality." With our fear of applying metrics to ministry, which has eternal significance, we leave the counting to the world of business, which has significance in this world only.

Accurately counting the right things can profoundly impact our ministry effectiveness. Knowing "the story in the stats" can help inform ministry decisions and lead us to do the most important things that produce the results that most please our Lord. Gathering and studying the right numbers can help us wisely invest our church's resources of time, effort, people, money, and facilities.

Jesus and His disciples counted. They knew how many He fed with the five loaves and fishes. When a crowd gathered, they often knew and recorded the number of men, women, and children present for the event. The early church counted. They knew that on the day of Pentecost "about three thousand were added to their number" (Acts 2:41). When Peter and John were jailed for their evangelistic success, they reported that about five thousand, not counting women and children, had become believers (Acts 4:4). In Berea it was reported that many Jews became believers as did some "prominent Greek women and many Greek men" (Acts 17:12). Upon returning from his first mission trip, Paul reported to the Council at Jerusalem that "many thousands of Jews have believed" (Acts 21:20). The early church clearly cared that many heard the gospel, many believed, and many were baptized.

Jesus counted, and the early church kept track of numbers. Therefore it is not unreasonable to expect churches today to use metrics to increase their effectiveness in doing God's work on earth. This book is designed to help churches increase their ministry effectiveness by helping church leaders measure the right things, in the best way, for the right reasons. This book deals with more than the mere *how* of measurement. Each chapter delineates a theology and philosophy designed to ensure that churches are measuring the right things for the right reasons.

The Excel spreadsheet file that you can download at www.abingdon-press.com is designed to make getting started simple. It contains a Metrics Manual to coach you in defining terms and understanding the basic measurement steps; the manual is also included as an appendix in the book. The spreadsheet provides basic template worksheets for performing the measurements discussed throughout the text. Text notes point to the related worksheets on the spreadsheet. While you will want to customize the templates to reflect your church's uniqueness, the templates provide a starting place.

CHAPTER ONE

THE FEAR OF NUMBERS

Seems Like Everyone Counts

In most of life's arenas, counting and keeping score seem second nature. We teach toddlers numbers by counting objects. Counting is often a child's first verbal skill. My grandchildren love to count the blocks they pile, one on top of the other, before they knock them down. Skipping rope and counting successful jumps seem to go hand-in-hand.

Children and bored adults count the cars on the train while waiting for it to pass. As teenagers, some friends and I climbed to the top of the Washington Monument. I counted each stair so I could brag about my "monumental" feat! Walkers and runners wear pedometers so they will know how many steps or strides they take during their workout. The more compulsive types around us count just about everything.

We keep track of the pennies in our piggy banks and the dollars in our IRAs. Athletes count runs, touchdowns, baskets, and seconds. Business leaders keep track of customers, costs, inventory, and sales, among a myriad of other things. Gamblers count cards and figure odds. Gallup and other pollsters will count just about anything if someone wants to know and will pay.

In business, sports, and politics, success demands that people not only count, but also count the right things and count them accurately. If a business stops counting the right things accurately, bankruptcy looms in its future. In sports, coaches and managers keep stats, study them, and make adjustments based on them. If they do not, their jobs will soon be in jeopardy. Tony La Russa, manager of the St. Louis Cardinals, is viewed as one of baseball's all-time best managers. Coincidentally he was one of the first to use a laptop computer in the dugout.

People count whatever is important to them. We count the money in our wallets or purses. Students calculate their grade point average. Since parents are loath to lose children, the parents of five do frequent head counts at the mall.

Churches Count, Too. Well, Sort of . . .

Failure to Count

Most churches count. Some do not, and not counting is always a bad sign. Not counting generally indicates they do not care or have given up. It's a little like children shooting hoops in the backyard with dad or mom. They know they can't win, so they want to *play for fun*. You know the tide is changing when they suddenly decide they want to keep score. That decision ushers in a period of close games with the parent still winning a good share of them. Then comes the stage when the parent is no longer interested in keeping score and wants to *play for fun*.

When doing a church assessment, we ask for statistics from the most recent ten-year period. Far too many churches struggle to assemble basic numbers like attendance, income, and baptisms. Gathering such elementary figures should never be a struggle unless the church has suffered a record-destroying fire, flood, or earthquake, or a crashed hard drive with no backup. Often the gaps in the data tell as much or more than the numbers themselves.

In my experience, the worse things are, the less people count. The more gaps in the data, the more bad years there have been. Keeping score was no longer fun, so they quit counting. When the statistics are bad and getting worse, they are depressing. Most people do not like feeling depressed. Making the changes necessary to reverse the negative trend can be difficult and requires giving up some things held dear by the church's long-timers. Since it is easier to stop counting than to make changes, they simply stop counting. Their inattention to numbers is a way of denying a reality they do not want to admit or address.

Lack of statistics for certain years sometimes indicates a kind of apathy. People counted and records were kept, but currently there is a new regime. The new pastor or new board did not care enough to protect the records and now they are lost. Or sometimes a long-time board that was unhappy with the former pastor will *lose* statistics, creating gaps in the records.

Since in our humanness we tend to count those things that matter most to us, most churches will at least count the offerings. They might not be able to tell you how many came to services, how many unbelievers became believers, how many participate in small groups, or how many serve in some form of ministry, but they can tell how much was given—and of course the amount given in these situations is never enough!

Failure to Count Accurately

Some churches count but do not do so accurately. Attendance figures are notoriously inaccurate. Since attendance is one of the things most frequently used to measure effectiveness, pastors and sometimes laypeople succumb to the temptation to count "everything that moves."

Over the years I have seen *attendance* figures that included not only worship but also Sunday school classes, the nursery, and even off-campus church retreats. Counting total Sunday attendance is neither bad nor unethical unless you compare your total Sunday attendance to your neighbor's worship only figure without disclosing the difference in methods.

There is a more common source of attendance inaccuracies found in churches with multiple worship services. The inflated attendance figures come when the same people are counted each time in multiple services. The same worship band, singers, worship leaders, ushers, greeters, and audio and video people often serve in multiple services.

Let's say on a given weekend a church has a team of six instrumentalists, six vocalists, two leaders for various aspects of worship, eight ushers, six greeters, two soundboard people, a slide projection operator, and the pastor running their worship services. That equals thirty-two people per service. If the same people serve in both services and are counted in both services, attendance figures for that day are inflated—by thirty-two. If they have three worship services, the inflation factor is sixty-four; and for four services, it's ninety-six!

There is a third fairly common cause of inaccurate counting. Since pastors are often ranked according to attendance figures, they have a bias for generosity when counting. When at a conference or convention, pastors are often asked, "How large is your church?" or as some put it, "How many are you *worshiping* these days?" One of the first questions search teams or call committees ask of any potential candidate is, "How large is your current church?" Pay raises tend to happen more frequently in churches where attendance is growing. All of this encourages pastors to speak "evange*last*ically" when citing attendance numbers.

A head usher who likes the pastor will allow generous attendance figures to stand. A head usher who really likes the pastor might even be compliant in the stretching of the figures, but woe to the pastor who falls from grace in the eyes of the head usher. Double counting ceases. New rules may appear such as, "If they aren't in their seat by five minutes after, they don't get counted." Actual counting may become less frequent, and *estimates* may become the norm. Of course these estimates tend to be significantly less than a hard count might produce and dramatically less than the pastor's tally.

Frequently when assessing a church we will be given *two sets of books*. The pastor (and/or supporters of the pastor) will provide one set of books showing strong attendance and perhaps even growth. The head usher, who often acts in collusion with or by order of a board at odds with the pastor, will provide a second set of books. Contrary to the pastor's books, these numbers will tell a different, more negative story. Sometimes neither set of numbers is accurate since both sides are "cooking the books" in order to support their purposes.

At some point, uncovering a fairly accurate attendance count is important in order to provide a helpful assessment. In the meantime, you know this for sure: Discovering two sets of books is a bad sign in either a business or a church. Finding them in a church suggests that there is bad blood between the pastor and some segment of the church.

Failure to Count the Right Things

Success in any endeavor requires that leaders count, count the right things, and count them accurately. Most churches do not count the right things.

I love baseball. My wife does not. She is a good sport, though, and humors me by attending about one game a decade. Some years ago, while pastoring a local congregation, I organized a group trip to the ball game. About forty people from our church signed up. Gwyn thought she would enjoy simply being with the people so she agreed to go. She brought along a book so she would have something to do when we all were engrossed in the game and the conversation lagged.

At one point in the game, one of baseball's most exciting plays unfolded. With a runner on first, the batter hit the ball sharply into the gap in right-center field. The ball rolled to the wall in the deepest part of the park. The runner was streaking from first and rounded third as the outfielder fired the ball to the relay man. Every person in the stadium (except Gwyn, of course) was on his or her feet in anticipation. The ball and runner reached home plate a split-second apart. The umpire signaled safe and the home team (our team) scored the go-ahead run. The stands went wild.

People began to sit down. The cheering died, and as sometimes happens after an exciting play the crowd became uncommonly quiet. At that very moment Gwyn looked up from her book and asked in a voice that could be heard by nearly all forty members of our group, "Who scored the touchdown?" She became an instant legend in her own time! At baseball games and at church, it is important to count the right things.

If churches count anything, nearly all of them will count two things. As one friend of mine puts it, "They count butts and bucks—how many people sat in the pews and how much money was placed in the offering plate." Or as another friend of mine puts it, "It's all about nickels, noise, and numbers."

The chapters that follow will deal extensively with the idea of counting the right things. I have come to believe firmly that it is vitally important for churches to count, "to keep score" if you please. Further, it is important to count accurately. Finally, it is essential, indeed critical, to count the right things.

Fear of Failure

So if counting is such a natural part of life and if keeping score is so important, then why do so many churches fail to count? Why do so many fail to count accurately, and why do so few count the things that matter most? Most often the problem is a matter of fear. To the degree the pastor or lay leaders harbor any doubt about their leadership effectiveness, they will have a similar degree of resistance to counting or keeping score. They fear their leadership effectiveness will be called into question. They fear they will be *found out* and labeled failures.

Over the years I have been told by many pastors and lay leaders that numbers do not measure spiritual success. I cannot recall a pastor or lay leader in a highly effective church ever expressing this sentiment. The fear of failure frequently expresses itself in a fear of accountability. Numerical measurement sets the stage for accountability.

In my twenty years of consulting with churches, I have observed the discomfort of many staff members as I talk about the importance of numeric measurement and the need to set numeric goals. They cringe when I get to the "M for Measurable" as I train in the use of SMART goals.[1] They have never before been held accountable for measurable outcomes, and they do not want to start now! They fear accountability because they fear the failure that measurable goals can expose. But it's delightful to see their dismay and discomfort dissolve as they come to realize they are always held accountable in some form and that the specificity of being held accountable to mutually agreed-upon, measurable goals can be a safe and productive place for them.

The Faithfulness vs. Fruitfulness Debate

Some churches, in their attempt to escape being accountable for effective ministry, hide behind God's call to be faithful. They cite the Bible's numerous calls to faithfulness. They excuse their lack of effectiveness by citing their faithfulness. They argue that God has called us to be faithful in our service.

God most certainly calls His followers to be faithful. In his first letter to the Corinthian church, the apostle Paul declared, "Now it is required that those who have been given a trust must prove faithful" (1 Corinthians 4:2). In his letters he specifically commended Timothy, Tychicus, Epaphras, and Onesimus for their faithfulness (1 Corinthians 4:17; Ephesians 6:21; Colossians 1:7; 4:7; 4:9). Paul made them heroes for the ages by naming them, and in the apostle's mind it was their faithfulness that made them heroes worth naming. Faithfulness is listed as a fruit of the Spirit (Galatians 5:22).

Those who seek to hide behind the call to be faithful often point to missionaries who labor a lifetime in a "hard field." "What about a missionary who works faithfully among people who practice another religion and in the end has no converts to show for his or her labor?" they ask. "Will you dismiss that missionary as a failure? Won't he or she hear the Lord say, 'Well done, good and faithful servant'?"

I cannot accept the *faithfulness* argument for two reasons. The first flows out of my own experience. I have never heard the "faithful missionary with no results" defense cited by a missionary. I have heard it cited by ineffective pastors and lay leaders here in the United States. I believe in the history of Christianity there have been, and are, people who have served faithfully with little or no tangible results to show for their labors, and I do believe they will be praised and rewarded generously by the Lord on Judgment Day. But few, if any, of us serving in the United States can cite with integrity the "hard field" as a reason for our ineffectiveness.

The second reason I cannot accept the *faithfulness* argument is far more substantive. The Bible clearly teaches that God expects us to be both faithful and fruitful.

The phrase, "Well done, good and faithful servant," is found in the parable of the talents (Matthew 25:14-30). In this story Jesus defines faithfulness *as* fruitfulness. True, He uses an economic rather than an agrarian metaphor, but He is talking about a form of fruitfulness. The two who produced a return on the Master's investment heard him say, "Well done, good and faithful servant" (21, 23). The non-productive servant was condemned as "wicked and lazy" (26). He was not commended for his faithfulness in the absence of fruitfulness.

One of Jesus' most powerful metaphors is that of the vine and the gardener (John 15:1-8 TNIV). "I am the true vine," Jesus declares. He admonishes us to remain in Him and promises that if we remain in Him, He will remain in us. Then He warns, "No branch can bear fruit by itself; it must remain in the vine. Neither can you bear fruit unless you remain in me" (4). He continues with His famous words, "I am the vine; you are the branches. If you remain in me and I in you, you will bear much fruit; apart from me you can do nothing" (5). He concludes by proclaiming, "This is to my Father's glory, that you bear much fruit, showing yourselves to be my disciples" (8). Can you imagine a more clear and profound call to fruitfulness?

In making His point unmistakably clear, Jesus reminds us of God the Father's role as gardener. He cuts off every branch that bears no fruit. It's not that if we are unfruitful, we might be in *danger* of being cut off. No;

He cuts off *every* unfruitful branch. Furthermore, He *prunes* every fruitful branch. Though I am not a fruit tree, I am sure that pruning is a painful process. I know His *pruning* in my life has always been painful! So why would our loving Father cause us pain? He makes us endure the pain of pruning "so that we will be even more fruitful." In the Divine Gardener's economy, it's all about fruitfulness.

Later in the same teaching session, Jesus said, "You did not choose me, but I chose you and appointed you to go and bear fruit—fruit that will last" (John 15:16). Our purpose in our lives as Christians is to bear fruit; fruit that will last for eternity. Now, that's a reason to get up in the morning! Can you imagine a more meaningful reason for living? I can't.

The Wisdom of Counting Now

Church leadership should never be taken lightly. Leadership in a church is a stewardship from God. We will be held accountable on that Day for what we have done with that stewardship. Just how productive were God's people under our leadership? Just how much return was realized on God's assets during our watch over them? Imagine trying to explain to God why the church under our leadership shrank at a time when spiritually hungry people desperately seeking to know Him surrounded us. Did the five talents He trusted to our care become ten, or did the two become four?

On that Day, we do not get "do-overs." When my older son was little and trying to do something new, each failure was accompanied by a request, "Do-over, Daddy?" On that Day there will be no do-overs. But by God's grace, each day of our ministry life is an opportunity to do it over, do it well, do it even more effectively.

By accurately counting the right things now, and working to improve our ministry effectiveness while we can, we increase the likeliness we will one day hear God say, "Well done, good and faithful servant." I think the "good" can be translated, "Well done, fruitful and faithful servant."

IF YOU COULD COUNT ONLY ONE THING

I magine a strange circumstance in which you were limited to counting just one thing as a measure of ministry effectiveness. What one thing would you count? For some, the choice would be as simple as choosing one of the two things they count presently—attendance or income. In most churches an interesting conversation would ensue—maybe even an argument. Should we measure small group participation? How about Bible reading or faithfulness in prayer? Some would argue for measuring Sunday school attendance. Others would opt for conversions. The longer the conversation and the more people involved, the longer the list would grow.

So if your church could measure its ministry effectiveness by only one statistic, what would you count? What measurement do you think is the most important one in God's eyes? What one stat would God check more than any other? Is there one measure that is more strategic than all others?

Count conversions. If you could count only one thing, you should count conversions. On the day of Pentecost, they did not count attendance. They counted conversions measured by baptisms (Acts 2:41).

What Matters Most to God?

Discerning God's Heart

God is a missionary God. He created us for fellowship with Him. Adam and Eve sinned, giving sin entrance into the life of every human being. As a consequence of Adam and Eve's sin, we are all born with a predisposition to sin. (See Romans 5; 1 Corinthians 15:22; Romans 3:23; Romans 6 [repeatedly describes us as "slaves to sin"]; and John 8:34.) Our sin severs us from the Holy God who cannot stand even a hint of sin, and fellowship with Him becomes impossible. It is impossible except for the intervention of the missionary God who sent His only Son whose death on our behalf makes reconciliation and renewed fellowship with God possible (Romans 5:10; 2 Corinthians 5:18-21; Colossians 1:22).

Peter, in his second letter, describes God as a patient God, not in a hurry to bring the world to its conclusion, "not wanting anyone to perish, but everyone to come to repentance" (2 Peter 3:9).

God's desire for fellowship with every person is so intense that He left heaven in the person of Jesus on a mission to restore us to fellowship with Him. Jesus came to earth "to seek and to save the lost" (Luke 19:10). Jesus Himself declared His primary mission to be calling "sinners to repentance" (Luke 5:32). He lived among us and lived like us in every way but one. He lived true to His character as God and lived without sin, thereby making Himself a worthy sacrifice on behalf of all people. Jesus was the only sacrifice sufficient to pay the price of human sin.

In his mentoring of young Timothy, the apostle Paul describes God as "our Savior who wants all people to be saved and to come to a knowledge of the truth." He then declares, "[T]here is one God and one mediator between God and human beings, Christ Jesus, himself human, who gave himself as a ransom for all people" (1 Timothy 2:3-6 TNIV).

So crucial to God's redemptive plan was Christ's death on the cross that one of history's great cosmic heavyweight championship fights between God and evil took place in the garden at Gethsemane (Matthew 26:36-45). Evil sought to exploit Jesus' natural human fear in order to interrupt God's great plan of grace and mercy. As He looked an excruciatingly painful death in the face, Jesus asked the Father to allow Him to escape that fate. Yet Jesus prayed, "My Father, if it is not possible for this cup to be taken away unless I drink it, may your will be done" (42). What was "the Father's will" for which Jesus was willing to die on the cross? It was the will of the missionary God who wanted a Way made so that humankind might once again have fellowship with Him (John 14:6).

The passion of God's heart is the redemption of all people to Himself. No wonder He counted conversions marked by baptisms on the day of Pentecost. In His economy, baptisms were the best way to measure the achievement of His heart's desire.

Discerning God's heart is one thing. Growing so that our hearts beat with His is another. And aligning our priorities and actions to reflect God's heart is still another. Could it be that the modern, Western churches' ineffectiveness in evangelism stems from the fact that our hearts do not beat with His? We fail to demonstrate any real passion for being agents of redemption from sin and reconciliation with God. Even when we value, preach about, and celebrate baptisms, we seldom count baptisms resulting from conversions separately or value them highly.

What might happen in your church if you began to share our Missionary God's passion for every person separated from Him by sin? What would change if you and your church became as singular as Jesus in your focus on seeking and saving the lost?

Hearing God's Command

Last words are often inspiring, sad, poignant, funny, profound, or defiant. Jesus' last words launched a movement.

> Then the eleven disciples went to Galilee, to the mountain where Jesus had told them to go. When they saw him, they worshiped him; but some doubted. Then Jesus came to them and said, "All authority in heaven and on earth has been given to me. Therefore go and make disciples of all nations, baptizing them in the name of the Father and of the Son and of the Holy Spirit, and teaching them to obey everything I have commanded you. And surely I am with you always, to the very end of the age." (Matthew 28:16-20)

Jesus' instruction to His followers and to the church could not be more focused. He did not offer us a menu from which we are free to choose what we like and leave what we do not like. The church does not get to choose from a smorgasbord of good things. To His followers and the church alike, He issues a clear, concise command, "Make disciples." As Christians we are to be consumed with making disciples. There is nothing more important in God's eyes for a church to do than to make disciples.

11

Certainly "making disciples" involves more than evangelism and conversions. In the Great Commission, Jesus brought two dimensions of disciple making into clear focus—baptizing and teaching. The purpose or the "end-game" of the teaching is not knowing but doing. Jesus said we should be "teaching them to obey everything I have commanded you" (20). Since Jesus commanded us to make disciples, obeying Him in everything requires our being effective in making disciples. Effective evangelism is not optional.

Some years ago, a denominational leader was speaking to a group of church leaders from various places in the United States. He passionately challenged them to lead their churches to effectiveness in evangelism. He declared his belief that baptisms are a key indicator of church health. Following his talk, a layman challenged him. "Our church has not baptized anyone in years," he said. "Are you saying my church is not healthy?"

Can a church be healthy if it is not making new disciples? Since we make new disciples by baptizing them and teaching them to obey, a church that is not baptizing is not being obedient to the command to make disciples. A church that fails to baptize and/or confirm new believers on a regular basis is not healthy. It is not effective. It may be *doing* church, but it is not *being* the church.

Measuring Conversions

Various Christian tribes measure spiritual milestones differently. Some traditions baptize infants, later training them up in the Christian faith, helping them affirm their own personal belief through confirmation. Other traditions dedicate infants later, baptizing them as children, teenagers, or adults upon their "profession of faith." Some practice adult conversion baptism while others practice adult conversion confirmation. Some welcome previously churched and baptized persons into membership without requiring either baptism or confirmation. Some require rebaptism.

My purpose here is not to discuss or debate the various beliefs and practices of different Christian churches. My purpose is twofold: first, to help churches strengthen their commitment to conversion growth and become more effective at evangelism, and second, to help establish some valid ways of measuring conversions.

Winning Our Own

Effective evangelism begins with helping our own children grow to know, love, and serve God. God entrusts children not only to nuclear families but to church families, expecting us to raise them up in the faith. Being raised in a Christian family and a Christian church should give a child a huge advantage in becoming a believer.

In baseball you are a star if you get a hit every third at bat, thereby hitting at a .333 pace. A utility infielder can bat .220 and still make millions. In God's economy, when it comes to winning our own, I believe it's God's intention that we bat 1,000 percent with our children.

No church I know measures up to such a standard. I doubt any has in the history of the church! But that fact does not change the validity of the goal. Why would we ever be happy with less than every child of the church becoming a baptized follower of Jesus who lives in obedience to God and alignment to what he or she has been taught from the Scriptures? We should plan for it, pray for it, work for it, and measure the degree to which we achieve the goal.

The first indication of our success in winning our own comes at confirmation or profession and baptism, since in both instances they affirm that the faith that has been passed on to them has become their own. We know that in either case the proof of true conversion comes only over time, through a life that gives evidence that faith in Jesus actually centers and shapes our lives. Though yet to be proved in the living, I think it is meaningful for a church to count either confirmation or profession of faith and baptisms as an indicator of evangelistic effectiveness. It is an indication of a church's effectiveness in winning its own.

Very few churches can tell you over time what percentage of their church children are confirmed or baptized upon their profession of faith. Most churches count how many, but they do not measure that number against the potential. What would the number be if every child of the church were to be confirmed or baptized as a professing believer? Churches simply do not keep track of this profoundly important statistic, even though they should.

If you choose to go beyond merely counting the number of children confirmed or baptized upon their profession of faith, what percentage should you seek to achieve? In a perfect world, you would make 100 percent your goal. But in the imperfect world in which we live, a challenging but practical minimum threshold might be two-thirds, or 66.6 percent.

The ultimate way to measure our effectiveness at winning our own would be to track the children and youth confirmed and/or baptized over time, recording evidence of lasting Christian commitment. Imagine how informative it would be if you were to measure, at five year intervals, just four things:

- Are they still attending worship regularly at your church or some other church?
- Are they participating in at least one small group?
- Are they currently involved in some aspect of mission or ministry?
- Are they currently serving in some form of professional Christian ministry such as pastor or missionary?

I know of no church that tracks the life evidence beyond confirmation or profession of faith and baptism. To the few who have even thought of it, the logistics have seemed daunting and they have opted not to measure long-term effectiveness in this way. The logistical hurdles are, however, surmountable and the value of knowing worth the effort.

Going Beyond Our Own

God also expects us to be effective in bringing unchurched and unbelieving people to faith in Him. He loves children and young people who have not been raised in a Christian environment. He wants them to come in faith to Him. God loves adults who have never been to church or have not yet learned who He is and decided to follow Him. God passionately desires that they learn of His love, forgiveness, and purpose for their lives. He is perpetually ready to help any and every church become more effective in evangelizing them.

In doing church assessments, I often calculate the *cost* of each conversion during the past year. By *cost* I mean how many attendees and how much money does it take to generate one conversion.[1] In one relatively short time frame I assessed a Baptist, a Presbyterian, and a Lutheran church.

The Baptist church baptized nineteen people during that year. Some were children and youth from church families; some were previously unchurched young people and adults who had recently professed faith in Jesus Christ. Based on their average worship attendance of 665, it took thirty-five attendees to generate one conversion marked by baptism. The church's total income for the same year was just over $1,486,000. The church spent $78,210 per conversion.

The Presbyterian congregation registered three baptisms. All were infant baptisms. Based on their average worship attendance of 216, it took seventy-two to generate one conversion. Their total income for the year was $811,663. They spent $270,554 per baptism that year.

The Lutheran church confirmed one hundred forty-eight people (sixty-eight junior and eighty adult confirmations). With worship attendance of 1,636, it took eleven worship attendees to generate one confirmation. This church values going beyond its own and emphasizes adult confirmations. It took an average of twenty attendees to produce each adult confirmation. The church's income was $5,787,219. The cost per confirmation was $39,102 and per adult confirmation, $72,340.

Each church must find its own comfort level when it comes to the spiritual "return on investment." While "return on investment" is a business term, I think it is an immensely helpful concept when it comes to measuring evangelistic effectiveness.

I am not suggesting you establish a financial threshold for the monetary cost per conversion. How can you put a cash value on an eternal soul? You cannot. A million dollars spent to bring one unbeliever to faith in Christ is worth it to that convert. But each church must decide if it is legitimate or even possible to spend a million per convert. Obviously, the goal here is to see the maximum number of converts for the least amount of dollars spent. In business terms, every church will want to maximize the return on the investment of their contributed dollars.

Effectively Reaching Beyond Our Own

How can we be more effective at going beyond our own? How can we be sure we are evangelizing more than mine and ours? If the way most Christians and churches typically evangelize generally results in so few transformed lives, then a whole new style of evangelism is needed in order to increase the number of converts.

I challenge churches to practice an approach I call "extreme" evangelism. "Extreme" evangelism is quite different from the typical evangelism practiced in most churches. Its target is not those already involved in church. It targets the unchurched and the unbelieving. These people are not found at church. They seldom even go near a church except for an occasional wedding or funeral. To get their attention and help them learn of God's love, forgiveness, and plan for their lives, you must practice a form of "in-their-neighborhood" evangelism because for the most part they choose not to visit yours. The purpose is to see unchurched and unbelieving people transformed into obedient followers of Jesus who become fully engaged participants in His mission and ministry.

Here are some distinctions between evangelism as usually practiced and "extreme" evangelism.

Characteristics of "Typical" Evangelism (Evangelism as Usual)	Characteristics of "Extreme" Evangelism (In-Their-Neighborhood Evangelism)

• Takes place on the church campus
  ○ Is evangelism by invitation
  ○ "Come to our worship multi-center, multi-purpose facility, or classroom . . ."
	• Takes place in the community
	  ○ Is evangelism by penetration
	  ○ "We will meet you where you work, study, play, meet, relax, and socialize."

• Occurs at times we set that are convenient to us	• Occurs at normal times in their schedules

• Is delivered in formats with which *we* are comfortable:
  ○ Worship services
  ○ Church events—pancake breakfasts, teas, special speakers from the Christian world
  ○ Programs—classes, small groups, athletic teams in the church league
	• Is delivered in formats with which *they* are comfortable:
	  ○ Movies, plays, and concerts
	  ○ Community events—block parties, city council meetings, kids' sports, school, political action meetings
	  ○ Relationships—most people do not need another meeting but can use another friend

• Content is verbal, with an emphasis on telling	• When content is verbal, it is more about listening and dialoguing
• Content is almost always verbal and cerebral	• Content is almost always behavioral, more about being and doing
• Focus is on my agenda, my message, and my desires for you	• Focus is on your interests, your wants, and your needs—including the spiritual
• A hard-to-do, frequently offensive religious activity	• A natural, pleasant, genuine, and effective way of living

Measuring Effectiveness in Reaching Beyond Our Own

The rule of thumb I hold up to the churches I coach is a *minimum* threshold of one conversion per ten worship attendees. If a church has an average weekly worship attendance of 300, it should aim for thirty adult conversion baptisms and/or adult conversion confirmations. If it averages 3,000, its *minimal* target should be 300 adult baptisms and/or confirmations.

The term *adult* is not used in a literal sense. It means a child, youth, or adult who has some degree of understanding about what it means to be a follower of Jesus, has decided to follow Jesus obediently, and has chosen to declare that decision through baptism and/or confirmation.

Functionally what this means is that, on the average, each attender would have to be used of God to help produce one conversion every ten years. Is this too much to expect? Is it enough to expect? The good news is that the God who wants all people to come to faith in Him will gladly help us overcome our failure and make our evangelistic efforts bear fruit.

HOW MANY AND HOW OFTEN?

There are a variety of cynical answers to the question, "What does measuring attendance accomplish?" If we did not measure worship attendance, how would pastors establish the pecking order when they meet? If I did not know that my church was larger than yours, on what basis would I feel superior to you? If we did not count worshipers, how in the world would we know if God was "blessing" our ministry and us? If we did not know that attendance is dropping, what rationale could we use to get rid of our pastor who is making changes we don't like?

Sadly, this cynicism has a basis in fact. We often measure *success* and *importance* by worship attendance. Who doesn't genuinely believe, at least in part, that Rick Warren is more important than a pastor who has labored for 20 years in a church of 125 in a town of 600?

What Does Measuring Attendance Accomplish?

Attendance *Does Not* Measure Importance

Any time we try to measure importance in terms of numbers, we are in trouble. There are too many variables and too many unknowns. Take evangelists for example. Reportedly, more than 500,000 people responded to Charles Finney's public invitations to receive Christ during his ministry as an evangelist:

During his meeting in Rochester, New York, the place was shaken to its foundations. Twelve hundred people united with the churches of Rochester Presbytery. All the leading lawyers, physicians, and business-men were saved. Forty of the converts entered the ministry, and the whole character of the town was changed. As a result of that meeting, revivals broke out in 1,500 other towns and villages.[1]

In his first year as an evangelist, Mordecai Ham saw more than 33,000 people make a public profession of their faith. Unlike Finney, whose ministry as an itinerant evangelist spanned only nine years due to poor health, Ham's ministry spanned decades. Reportedly, over 300,000 people responded to Ham's public invitations. Finney influenced lawyers, physicians, and businessmen. Ham certainly touched the lives of some elite, but he was most well known for touching the lives of regular and needy people. One close observer stated, "Under his preaching I have seen murderers saved, drunkards converted, homes reunited, and men and women dedicate their lives for special service."[2]

Which evangelist was more important? Who had the greater impact? Finney recorded more professions of faith. He likely touched the lives of more influential community leaders than Ham. How can one measure the ripple effect of the forty converts who entered ministry and the revivals in 1,500 other towns and villages?

Mordecai Ham's impact in touching the poor, needy, alcohol addicted, and criminals was admirable and no doubt had a great impact on those lives and the lives of many people around them. One could assume that Charles Finney was the more important evangelist because he recorded more decisions for Christ and touched the lives of more influential people. That assumption could be challenged by the fact that at a November 1934 evangelistic meeting in Charlotte, North Carolina, a young man named Billy Graham responded to the invitation given by Mordecai Ham and decided to follow Jesus and serve Him for a lifetime.

Both were profoundly important in shaping the religious landscape of America for more than a century. Both had immeasurable importance to every person whose life was affected by their preaching. Both had a ripple effect that can be measured accurately only in eternity. Comparing numbers does not establish relative importance or value.

Attendance *Does Not* Measure Success

Some love to use numbers to measure success. If my attendance figures are going up, I am succeeding. If thousands attend my church, I am a success. Granted, it would be foolish to argue that declining attendance is a sign of success.

Some years ago, my parents attended a church in Florida. When they started attending, the church's average worship attendance was around three hundred and growing. Because of his *success*, the pastor was an attractive potential candidate for the search committee of a larger church. The committee pursued him, and he succumbed to the call to "bigger and better things."

After some time, my parents' church called a new pastor. Both his perspective and his preaching were negative. Weekly scolding from the pulpit began to take its toll. He loved books more than people. He hibernated in his study. He seldom met with, visited, or even talked to people between Sunday mornings. His theology was far narrower than his predecessor's, and his lifestyle *rules* were many and restrictive.

Within eighteen months he had *grown* the church of three hundred worshipers to about sixty per Sunday. Someone finally had the nerve to tell him he was not succeeding as pastor of that church. He disagreed, arguing that his had been a ministry of "cleansing" and that he had inherited a church full of carnal Christians who were not living a "truly Christian life." He believed God had sent him to the church to *purify* the church and work with the "faithful remnant." No one else considered him successful. Not even the faithful remnant considered him a success. They ultimately fired him just about the time they could no longer pay him. The church never recovered from that pastor's *successful* ministry and soon closed its doors.

The fact that declining numbers do *not* indicate success does not mean that growing numbers *do* indicate success. Not all growth is healthy. Not all large churches are successful in accomplishing God's will on earth. Some large churches do nothing for their communities except take up space and use public services for which they pay no taxes. Gathering a growing crowd does not necessarily define success. Many televangelists in the midst of scandal and corruption have been able to gather a crowd.

If attendance is not a reliable measure of importance or success, why count? If worship attendance can give so many "false positives," why emphasize counting attendees? What does tracking worship attendance accomplish anyway?

Attendance *Does* Measure Influence

Attendance can be a helpful measure of influence. A church averaging seven hundred in worship attendance is obviously influencing more people than a church that averages one hundred fifty. This simple fact, however, does not address the extent, the quality, or the nature of the influence. It's a quantitative, not qualitative measure of influence. The issue of measuring influence qualitatively will be addressed in later chapters.

Attendance as a quantitative measure of influence, however, can help us increase ministry effectiveness.[3] A desire for growth can be healthy and highly motivating. It's a good thing to desire numeric growth when that desire is motivated by a drive to influence a growing number of people for Christ. Longing to help an ever-increasing number of people serve the King by ministering "unto one of the least of these" (Matthew 25:40) is a good thing. Who could find any fault with desiring to help more and more people discover the riches of God's grace, the love of Jesus, and the power of the Holy Spirit?

Wanting to influence others to do our will and to serve our purposes flies in the face of Jesus' teaching and example. But wanting to influence others for their benefit and for their fulfillment is pleasing to our Lord. The apostle Paul burned with a passion to influence others. As Timothy's mentor, Paul expected Timothy to follow his example. Paul wanted his life to influence Timothy for Timothy's good and for the sake of the young man's ministry.

Paul not only urged Timothy to follow his mentor's example but also urged him to be an influence on others. In his second letter to Timothy he said, "And the things you have heard me say in the presence of many witnesses entrust to reliable people who will also be qualified to teach others" (2 Timothy 2:2 TNIV). He was calling Timothy to influence others by his teaching.

Paul further instructed Timothy to influence others by his life: "Don't let anyone look down on you because you are young, but set an example for the believers in speech, in life, in love, in faith and in purity" (1 Timothy 4:12).

In his final commissioning of Timothy, Paul urged, "In the presence of God and of Christ Jesus, who will judge the living and the dead, and in view of his appearing and his kingdom, I give you this charge: Preach the Word; be prepared in season and out of season; correct, rebuke and encourage— with great patience and careful instruction" (2 Timothy 4:1-2). Influence them by your preaching—correct, rebuke, and encourage. Sounds like a mandate to influence others in Jesus' name and for Jesus' sake.

So use worship attendance to help gauge the extent of your church's influence and cultivate a passion to see your attendance grow so your church can influence an ever-increasing number of people for Kingdom purposes.

Attendance *Does* Measure Trends

Discovering trends by measuring worship attendance can also help you become more effective in leading your church. I remember being called in to consult with a conflicted church some years ago. The pastor had been at the church for about two years. The board was pounding away on the pastor's soul and psyche because worship attendance was declining. It was his fault, they asserted. He had grown his previous church, and they had called him there to help this church grow. He wasn't getting the job done.

A quick check of the attendance figures confirmed that worship attendance was declining. A look farther back revealed that the church's worship attendance had been in decline for fifteen years! All but two of the board members had been in leadership in that church for more than a decade. The downward trend in attendance clearly predated the current pastor, a fact the pastor had pointed out with no effect. In fact, we discovered a second trend in the attendance figures. The decline in worship attendance had been moderating for over eighteen months, and for the past six months the attendance had nearly plateaued.

What conclusions could be drawn from the trends discovered in the worship attendance figures? First, the common denominator in the past decade's decline was the board, not the pastor. If leadership was to blame for the church's decline, the blame should be laid at the feet of the board members.

Second, the pastor was succeeding in reversing a fifteen-year trend. He deserved applause, praise, and support rather than the pummeling he was receiving. The church would have been better served had the board members been analyzing, with the pastor, the factors that were contributing to the early stages of reversing the slide. The lay leaders should have been working with the pastor to find additional, even more effective ways of attracting new people to worship.

Just noting the trend is not enough. It's coming to understand the underlying contributors to the trend. If worship attendance is increasing, what is fueling the increase? Can those things be improved upon or expanded? What else can be done to further increase the positive momentum and therefore the church's influence? Can the growth trend be made stronger?

A declining trend requires a similar analysis. How steep is the decline? What are the contributing factors? What changes must be implemented if the trend is to be reversed? Reversing a negative trend always requires change. In fact a negative trend is often the result of an unwillingness to change. The definition of insanity is, as the old saying goes, "continuing to do the same things and expecting different results." The steeper the negative trend, the more radical the changes and the quicker they must be implemented.

Good leaders know the trends. Wise leaders understand the underlying causes of the trends. Effective leaders are always making changes, sometimes subtle, sometimes drastic, in order to perpetuate or strengthen a positive trend or to intercept and reverse a negative trend.

Attendance *Does* Measure Outward Focus

Growth in worship attendance means that new people are being reached and attracted to the church. Plateaued worship attendance means that the same folks are stopping by again and again on Sunday mornings. There will be a few new faces to offset those who move, get mad and leave, get sick and cannot attend anymore, or die. Declining worship attendance indicates that few, if any, new people are being attracted to the church and that people who formerly attended are no longer showing up on Sunday.

The addition of new people always creates growing attendance figures. The more outward focused the church, the more new people will materialize. Outward focus means intentionally doing things to attract new people. Outward focus means prioritizing activities and ministries that reach out to new people, touching them where they live, work, and play.

In conducting an assessment in a clearly inward focused church, I asked the question, "What specific things are you doing to reach the unchurched and unbelieving people in your neighborhood and community?" One man responded, "We open the doors and turn on the lights every Sunday morning." Sadly, that is the extent of the outward focus in far too many churches.

Understanding Outward Focus

What does it mean to be outward focused? Inward focus is always about the people who are *already here*; outward focus is about those who are *not here yet*. The *already here* include current believers, members, and attendees. The *not here yet* include the unbelieving, the unchurched, and potential attendees. Some people assume being outward focused means ignoring the people who are already here in favor of those who are not yet here.

Ignoring those who are already part of the church would be to discount what it means to be a church. Christ intends for the church to be a place where His followers are taught (Acts 2:42), encouraged (1 Thessalonians 5:11; Hebrews 3:13; 10:25), cared for (Galatians 6:2), and empowered to serve (Romans 12:7; 1 Peter 4:10; 5:2-3).

In the first-century church:

> All the believers were one in heart and mind. No one claimed that any of their possessions was their own, but they shared everything they had. With great power the apostles continued to testify to the resurrection of the Lord Jesus. And God's grace was so powerfully at work in them all that there were no needy persons among them. From time to time those who owned lands or houses sold them, brought the money from the sales and put it at the apostles' feet, and it was distributed to anyone who had need. (Acts 4:32-35 TNIV)

How many churches do you know that even begin to resemble the example of the early church's care for those within the body? I personally know of none. The degree to which the early church in Jerusalem cared for their own flies in the face of our Western culture of individualism and right to private ownership.

Furthermore, ignoring those who are already a part of the church would be silly. They are the ones who enable the church to effectively reach those who are not yet believers or churchgoers. The people are the church, and, as we will see in a subsequent chapter, without their involvement the church will never achieve maximum effectiveness. So being outward focused does not mean ignoring those who are already part of the church.

Inward focus and outward focus are not mutually exclusive. Both are found in healthy churches. Both are requirements for effective ministry. So what makes a church outward focused as opposed to inward focused? Outward focus is simply, profoundly, and always a matter of *priority*.

Here it is in a nutshell. When a church cannot do both, the outward focused church will always choose to do what is best for those who are not yet there. Whenever a church cannot simultaneously do what is best for the people who are already there and the people who are not yet there, the outward focused church will always choose to do what is best for the unbelieving, the unchurched, the de-churched, or the under-churched.

You will know you are outward focused when you do not have enough money, people, space, or time and you choose to do what's best for the unbelieving and the unchurched. Imagine a church where the Longtimers' Sunday school class has met in the same room for decades. They once filled the room that holds eighty people. Now there are eight to ten on a good Sunday. Imagine in that same church a class of new attendees, most of whom are new Christians because of the church's effective evangelistic ministry. The new-attendee/new-Christian class has outgrown its current room, and the only larger classroom *belongs* to the Longtimers. Imagine the church's leaders summoning up the courage and asking the Longtimers' class to move to a smaller room in order to accommodate the growing new-attendee/new-Christian class. Now you are imagining an outward focused church when the Longtimers gladly make the change, rejoicing because God is blessing their church with growth. Of course, many of us can *only* imagine such a thing happening in our church.

To sum up, attendance figures are not reliable measures of importance or success, but they can be helpful in assessing relative influence, tracking trends, and indicating the degree to which a church is outward focused. How should you count in order to reap these benefits?

There's More Than One Way to Measure

Attendance as a Measure of Breadth

The most basic use of attendance as a measure of breadth is simple: the more people in attendance, the broader the influence of the church.

Generally speaking, a church with seven hundred fifty in worship on Sunday has a wider influence than one with one hundred fifty in attendance. It's that simple. It's that direct.

The Concept of Market Share

There are two additional ways to look at worship attendance that can offer even greater insight into a church's breadth of influence. The first is to compare worship attendance to the population of the church's geographic parish area. Calculating this percentage gives a more accurate indication of a given church's breadth of impact in its community. Let me illustrate.

Saddleback Church in Lake Forest, California, averages around twenty-three thousand attendees per weekend. Clearly, Saddleback has a profound breadth of influence in Orange County. By sheer force of its weekend worship attendance alone, Saddleback is one of the top five most influential churches in America.[4] But to what extent does it effectively penetrate its geographic parish area? According to census data released by the state of California in 2005, Lake Forest's population was 77,859. One could argue that about 29.5 percent of Lake Forest attends worship at Saddleback on an average weekend. While that would be impressive, it would be wrong. Saddleback's geographic parish area extends far beyond Lake Forest. The population of the seven adjacent towns and cities is 538,508.[5] A more accurate assessment of Saddleback's market share in its "neighborhood" is 4.2 percent.

By comparison it would be easy to dismiss the influence of Bethel Baptist Church in Hayes Center, Nebraska. Hayes Center is a village named for President Rutherford B. Hayes. It is the county seat for Hayes County. Its estimated population in 2003 was 248. The entire county's estimated population in 2004 was 1,115. Average attendance at Bethel Baptist is currently about sixty-two. In market share terms, that's 25 percent of Hayes Center and 5.6 percent of Hayes County attending worship at Bethel.

While Saddleback's breadth of influence is clearly worldwide, this little church's span of influence, or its share of its local church market, is almost identical to Saddleback. Though it would be foolish to argue that the breadth of influence for both churches is the same, both churches are equally effective in influencing their geographic parish area given their context and potential. But for either megachurch or small town parish the goal should be the same: increase market share!

Market share is a term well known in the business world. Every astute business leader knows the company's market share at any given time. Every progressive company will have a plan to increase its market share in the future.

What would happen if churches began to think about market share? What if your church knew the percentage of the market you were already reaching and had a goal and a plan to reach a greater percentage of the potential market in the future? What might happen if you as church leaders got on your knees before God and asked, "What percentage of our neighbors do You want us to influence for You in the future?" What if you prayed that prayer until you had a consensus on a percentage from God? How much of your community does God want your church to touch, to influence in His name and for His sake?

A Reflection of Your Community

There is a second way to look at worship attendance that offers a greater insight into a church's breadth of influence. Simply stated it is this: How well do your worship attendance figures reflect the cultural, ethnic, and economic make-up of your community?

Some years ago, I had the privilege of working with a church in the Los Angeles area that once dominated its city. Its attendance exceeded a thousand in a day when a thousand was considered a megachurch. It sat on a high-profile site on a main thoroughfare. The church was still the largest non-governmental landowner in its city, but its worship attendance had dwindled to the mid-four hundred range. Attendees were virtually all white and increasingly middle-aged and older.

One day, the church's leaders noticed something. Very few of their neighbors looked like them. Most did not speak English. A quick check of the demographics confirmed the observations. The overwhelming majority of their neighbors were Hispanic and Vietnamese. The church's current attendees were no longer a reflection of their community. They were in danger of becoming a dead, old "First Church" consisting of a handful of white-skinned, white-haired folks rattling around in a massive old sanctuary.

To their credit, the leaders recognized that people who looked like them and spoke only English could not effectively reach their new neighbors. They began to pray that God would bring to them catalytic leaders from the Hispanic and Vietnamese communities who could lead them in effectively reaching the people who now live in the community. Within the next four years, the church launched a successful Hispanic congregation, a successful Vietnamese congregation, and a fledgling Farsi congregation. Interestingly, attendance at the Anglo worship service began growing as well. Now, more than fifteen years later, this church is a vibrant influence in its community rather than a musty old "First Church." It once again mirrors the cultural and ethnic make-up of its community.

Analyzing the ethnic, cultural, and economic make-up of your attendees in relationship to the make-up of your community helps you know the breadth of your influence across the diverse demographic that is your neighborhood.

Attendance as a Measure of Depth

When counted and analyzed properly, attendance can give you an effective way to look at the commitment and, perhaps, the maturity of your congregation. You can get a partial measure of the depth of a person's commitment to your church by tracking the percentage of Sundays he or she actually attends worship. The assumption behind this thinking is simply this: there is a positive correlation between spiritual maturity and heeding the biblical admonition, "Let us not give up meeting together, as some are in the habit of doing, but let us encourage one another—and all the more as you see the Day approaching" (Hebrews 10:25).

In years past, people were far less mobile. They stayed home on weekends and vacationed for a week or maybe two every summer. People were home on Sundays, and they went to church. Though I long ago forgot his name, I can still see in my mind's eye an elderly gentleman who was revered by all as he tottered around my childhood church. He was noticeable because of his frailty and the curvature of his spine. He always wore a suit and tie, and from the lapel of his jacket hung four long rows of medals. They were his perfect attendance pins! Our church gave medals for perfect attendance, which was defined as fifty or more Sundays per year. This man was well into his eighties and had attended our church all his life. He had collected nearly eighty of those medals. We children feared that his back was bent from the weight of his medals, and we vowed never to accumulate them in order to avoid his fate. He was the closest I have ever come to knowing a true 100-percenter!

How many churches still give out perfect attendance medals? How many people are in town fifty or more Sundays a year? How many have a rhythm of life that says, "You'll find me in church every Sunday unless I am in the hospital or dead"? We live in a different day. Today many people consider themselves *regular* church attendees if they are there 50 percent of the time.

The simple fact is this. The more frequently a person attends worship, the more opportunity a church has to influence his or her spiritual life. If the church uses its worship time wisely, it can be a catalyst for spiritual growth and depth in the lives of the attendees. It stands to reason that over time, a church will see greater spiritual depth in those who attend 90 percent of the time than in those who attend 25 percent of the time.

If you have an interest in increasing your church's effectiveness in helping develop spiritual maturity in your constituents, you will aggressively seek ways to increase the participation of your people in the ministries of your church. Participation in aspects of church life other than worship, such as Sunday school, small groups, and ministry involvement, also impact spiritual depth. (Measuring these areas will be addressed in subsequent chapters.) Seek to increase participation in each of these areas, but know that increasing the frequency of worship attendance will always be a significant means of increasing spiritual depth.

Measuring depth by measuring attendance is dividing your church's average weekly worship attendance by the church's total number of constituents.[6] Few churches know their total number of constituents. They think only in terms of attendance and membership. Identifying the total number of constituents first requires defining what you mean by *constituent*. A good working definition is "those who live in your parish geographical area and who attend worship at least four times a year." A once or twice a year attendee is probably not yet a constituent. Using "at least four times a year" as a threshold gets you past your Christmas- and Easter-only visitors.

Calculate the average percentage of worship attendance per constituent.[7] Use that figure as your base line. Set a goal that is significantly higher than your base line. Strategize numerous and highly intentional ways to raise the percentage. Work your plan, and in time you will see evidence of greater spiritual depth and maturity.

CHAPTER FOUR

HOW MANY STAY?

When my boys were small, we took a family trip to Estes Park, Colorado. Not far from where we were staying was a stocked pond. My older son enjoyed fishing and begged me to take him. I took both sons but upon arrival discovered it was a "catch and release" operation.

Catch and release just did not float my boat. What's the sense of catching a fish only to let it go? My father was an avid fisherman. My family was not rich. We were not even middle-class. We always had more love than money and so I never describe my upbringing as poor, but my mother constantly had to find ways to stretch a dollar. So my father's fishing was both a hobby and a food source. We kept and cleaned the fish we caught. Catch and release was not in my vocabulary. Although I never shared my father's passion for fishing, I went along because I wanted to be with him. For me the joy of fishing was time with my father and the wonderful fresh fish dinner that always followed.

I took my boys, left that place, and traveled a short distance to another location. This one was similar—stocked pond, all gear provided, no license needed—but this was a "catch and cook" operation. My sons enjoyed the fishing. I enjoyed the eating.

"Catch and release" is what many churches do with visitors. That makes even less sense to me than "catch and release" fishing.

Isn't Visitor Retention Obvious?

Visitor Retention's Undeniable Importance

Attracting and keeping visitors are fundamental to growth. A church that never has visitors will never grow; it will, in fact, die over time. Very few churches *never* have visitors. Nearly every church, by virtue of having at least some visitors, has the potential to gain new attendees and members. A church that has visitors but never retains any of them will never grow. It too will die over time.

At least some rudimentary level of visitor retention is required for a church simply to remain plateaued. Natural attrition—by death, by members moving, and by people deciding to go to another church or simply stop going to church—contributes to decline that requires new people to offset. Even if a church does not want to grow, it must still retain visitors to stay alive!

Retaining visitors is the easiest way to grow. When visitors show up at your church, the hard work is over. It is much more difficult to get the attention of the unchurched and unbelieving and to convince them to come to your church building than to keep them once they come. In my experience of working with many churches, most church leaders consider assimilation difficult. Church after church wants help in assimilation. Even more disconcerting is how many churches are ineffective at assimilation and do not want help!

Visitor retention ought to be a priority for every church. Why not get good at the easiest method of gaining new attendees and members? It seems so obvious.

Why Do So Many Fail at the Obvious?

Since it seems so obvious you would think keeping visitors would be toward the top of every church's *to-do* list. But you would be wrong. Time after time in doing assessments or consultations, I will ask, "What's your visitor retention rate?" In some instances an explanation is required. "What do you mean, 'retention rate'?" The vast majority of churches, even the ones that understand the question, do not know what percentage of visitors they are retaining. Their eyes avert upwards as they think, as if they are counting visitors in their mind's eye. The answer almost always begins, "Well, I think it might be around…"

Sometimes they cover their embarrassment by asking a question instead of answering mine. "So what do you mean by 'visitor'?" Dig the hole a little deeper. If you have not defined what a visitor is, you definitely do not know how many you are retaining. If tracking visitor retention is so obviously important, why do the majority of churches fail to do it?

A *Fear of Failure*

Intuitively, many pastors and lay leaders know their church is doing poorly at retaining visitors. If you are tracking visitor retention and not retaining many or maybe even any, your failure in this area is declared in the figures. Since it's a whole lot easier to stop counting or never begin counting in the first place than to do an effective job at assimilation, many churches simply choose not to count.

Retaining 30 percent or more of your visitors is hard work. It seldom "just happens." A church has to do such hard and tedious work as:

- Discovering who your visitors are,
- Following up on them,
- Creating and maintaining numerous effective entry point ministries that make it easy for new people to find relationships and a place in the church, and
- Tracking the visitor's progression through the steps to fully assimilated status.

This is not easy. It requires energy and effort every single week. It's too hard and too tedious for most churches. Yet if you do not do these things, and more, you will have a very low retention rate. And if you are not willing to do all these things, it is better not to count at all because, if you do count, it will be public knowledge that you are failing, and who wants that?

A *Fear of Growth*

Some churches fail to retain visitors because they really do not want them to stay around. The people who are already there like it as it is. They believe growth will change things for the worse, not for the better.

When fear is a factor in a plateaued or declining church, peel back the fear to its core, and you will discover it's not really a fear of growth; it's a fear of loss. There are those for whom the church is their extended family. At the church's present size, they can know and be known by everyone.

Theirs is a "Cheers Church"—a place where everybody knows your name. "If our church grows," they say, "we will lose our sense of family." They resist going to two services even though the seats are filled at worship. They are unmoved by the plea, "We must add a second service if we are to grow." Growing is the last thing they want. "If you go to two services, you will divide our church," they argue. The real problem is if the church goes to two services, they will not be able to know everyone and, more importantly, everyone will not know them. Though small group participation, not worship, is the most effective creator of community, many participants in "Cheers Churches" reject the small group solution and stubbornly argue against multiple services.

Others fear the loss of power and control. They hold key positions, and from those "places of service" they can control much of what happens in the church. Perhaps more accurately, they can stop the church from doing the things they do not want done. They are key opinion leaders, each with their constituencies whom they both shape and represent. Their constituencies keep them in power. If too many new people show up and get involved, their constituencies are diminished in importance and voting power. Growth threatens their influence, position, and control. The motivation may be for sheer power, or they may be reluctant to give up influence and control because they do not trust others to make good decisions. They define good decisions, of course, as the decisions they would make.

Unwillingness to Change

Another common reason that certain churches do not want visitors to stick is that the people who are already there know that new people will inevitably bring new ways of doing things. In most plateaued or declining churches, members have already tried to attract people *like them*, who will want things as they already are. The problem is, there are too few people who like to worship the way they do, sing the songs they sing, or meet at the times they meet for the reasons they meet. The majority of people in these churches value things the way they are. They are focused more on leaving things the way they like them than on making changes that might attract more visitors. When visitors do come—unless they are just like the existing members—the members do not want them to stay.

A cynic once said, "Churches are very willing to change. They will make any change necessary to keep things the same!" While humorous, the statement is far too true to be funny.

The Root Cause

There is a common root for the fear of failure, fear of growth, and an unwillingness to change. The common root is the absence of passion for lost people.

Some years ago, I was asked to consult with a group about which I had only a limited knowledge at the time. As a denomination this group had a reputation for a strong commitment to the Bible as God's Word, but was also known for a marked lack of evangelistic effectiveness. The district staff with whom I was working was deeply disturbed by the evangelistic ineffectiveness of their churches. We worked at articulating clear mission and vision statements that could guide the district staff in their planning and activities. They stated their mission in these words:

> "The mission of the district ministry team is to partner with member congregations and their leaders as they nurture disciples and reach the lost."

Their vision statement became:

> "We see every congregation and ministry of the district effectively reaching the lost."

Shortly after they settled on their mission statement and, while they were preparing their plan to achieve it, I was conducting focus groups throughout the district. One evening I met with a group of twenty lay leaders from eight congregations. Through the evening a recurring theme emerged. When asked what the church's greatest ministry challenge was, every single person cited the lack of growth. All eight congregations were in decline. It seemed that no matter what question I asked, before long the group was telling me again about declining attendance and membership.

At the end of the evening, I mentioned that the district staff had completed the writing of a mission statement and asked if the group would like to hear it and give the staff some feedback. Without hesitation, all agreed to stay. I wrote the statement on a white board, "The mission of the district ministry team is to partner with member congregations and their leaders as they nurture disciples and reach the lost." The room was silent. Finally someone said, "Do they have to use the word 'lost'? That seems so harsh."

The room erupted in animated discussion. It was unanimous; calling people "lost" was not a good thing. Could the staff say it in a less offensive way? I listened as all who chose to speak affirmed the feeling that "lost" was not a good word choice. After a time, I asked a question in order to make an observation. "Think back over the evening," I said. "What was the common thread that ran through all the subjects we talked about this evening? What was the common denominator in every church represented here tonight?"

They thought for a moment, and then one person said, "Our congregations are not growing." I then asked my question. "Do you think there might be a correlation between the fact your churches are not growing and the fact you find it so difficult to call lost people *lost?*" "Now it was already quite late, and some had driven quite a distance to attend—but no one left. There was an energetic conversation for the next half hour resulting in agreement that maybe there was a correlation and maybe the staff mission statement had merit.

Long experience has convinced me that churches whose leaders truly believe that unbelieving people are in real danger of spending eternity apart from God in hell are the churches that have a passion to touch the lives of unbelieving people with the Good News of God's love and Jesus' sacrifice on the cross. It is the conviction that Jesus is the only means of salvation and way to eternal life that causes these churches to focus on evangelism and do effective assimilation (John 11:25; 14:6-7; Acts 4:8-12; 10:43; Galatians 1:4; 1 Timothy 2:5-6; 1 John 5:20). The stakes are high enough in their minds to successfully counteract their fear of failure, growth, and change.

The Functional Cause

There are churches that do not fear growth. They are willing to change, sometimes even drastically, if it will help them reach more unchurched, unbelieving people. They have a genuine passion for lost people. But they still fail to effectively retain visitors. Why is that? What's the problem?

The answer is almost always the absence of an *effective system of assimilation.* What passes for assimilation in most churches are a few occasional or periodic events like visitors' luncheons; "Get Acquainted" classes; new members' orientation classes; or the Saddleback model of 101, 201, 301, and 401 classes. While a good assimilation system will likely include these or similar activities, these events in and of themselves do not constitute a system.

At this point it is enough to simply note the problem. A later section of this chapter will address the creation and operation of an effective system of assimilation.

The Indispensable Mind-set

Getting More Fish to Swim to Your Aquarium

There is a common mind-set found in churches that are effective in visitor retention. It flows from the theological conviction that lost people are lost. That conviction finds expression in two behavioral mindsets. The first is that these churches have an absolute passion to get more fish to swim to their aquarium. The second is that they are intent on keeping every fish that comes their way. They are not interested in transferring fish from one aquarium to another. For them, it's all about catching new fish. In short they have both evangelism and assimilation on their minds, and they work at being highly effective at both.

Assimilation and evangelism are almost inseparable. An effective system of assimilation begins with an evangelistic heart. An evangelistic heart is passionate about developing relationships with unbelieving people in order to become a bridge over which people can walk to find a relationship with Christ. A church with an evangelistic heart is passionate about intersecting the lives of unbelieving, unchurched people. The church's leaders want more people to come under the church's regular, ongoing influence in order to help them become mature followers of Jesus.

Why is this outward focused, evangelistic mind-set so crucial to an effective retention ministry? Simply put, the more visitors you have, the more visitors there are to retain. Conceivably a church could have a retention rate of 75 percent over the course of a ministry year. If, however, they had only four visitors that year, we would applaud them for assimilating three of the four, but we would prefer to see them retain 75 percent of fifty visitors in a year. In most instances we would prefer to see a 50 percent retention rate of fifty visitors than a 100 percent rate with four visitors. Effective assimilation systems always begin with increasing the number of visitors. Assimilation starts with getting more fish to swim to your aquarium.

Attraction as a Strategy

The most frequently used strategy in most churches is attraction. Churches plan events in order to attract the unchurched and unbelieving. These include special speakers, concerts, Christmas extravaganzas, Easter pageants, elegant women's teas and fashion shows, and father and son breakfasts with a famous athlete or coach.

Since churches that plan and hold these kinds of events have learned that no amount of advertising causes flocks of people to come, their regular attendees and members are admonished to bring their unchurched friends. The operative word is *bring*. If one brings an unchurched person, he or she is, by definition, *coming* to the event. It's an attraction strategy.

Intentionally trying to attract people to church is not a bad thing. In far too many churches, attracting new people is not a priority. They are satisfied doing "the same old, same old" for the same old people. It has been years since their leaders have had a serious focus on intentionally doing things that would attract new people. They might have had some conversations about it, but none that have resulted in actually doing something to attract unchurched and unbelieving people. Of course, none of these churches are growing.

Attraction events can be a good thing, especially if they are attractive to the unchurched. A widespread problem is that churches often plan these events without ever consulting the people they are trying to attract. These events are planned and carried out by a group of people who have been part of the church (or some church) for years—maybe even their entire lives. They haven't been unchurched in years. Many of them are so busy with family, work, and church that they hardly know an unchurched person. They are acquainted with hundreds but have never engaged any of them in a significant conversation about church or what might actually attract an unchurched person to church.

In the business world, the most profitable companies frequently ask for input from their customers and potential customers. They ask what people like about their product. They ask how their product could be made better. They hold focus groups, do market tests of their products, and seek the input of those who already use their product and more important, the input of people who could one day become a customer. If companies do this in order to make a few dollars, maybe churches should do it in order to impact more lives for time and eternity.

Attraction events that are planned with input from the kind of people you are trying to attract will likely be more successful than ones planned in ecclesiastical isolation. A wise person once said, "It is not according to the taste of the angler, but according to the taste of the fish that one baits the hook." Watching my father try to think like a fish in order to use the right lure, the right fly, and the right tasty treat on the hook always amused me. Whether ocean or lake fishing, my dad always watched for clusters of boats. I learned an immutable law of fishing, "Where the boats gather, the fish are biting." Upon joining a gathering of boats my dad would always call to the nearest fishermen, "What are they biting on?"

In church life we have a great advantage; the *fish* we are seeking can speak. If we just ask the right questions and listen to their answers, they will inevitably tell us what they are biting on.

Even the best use of attraction as a strategy to reach new people is not enough. The problem with attraction is it's not the most effective means of reaching new people. People have plenty of things to do already. They do not need one more place to go. They are already living margin-less lives with overflowing appointment books and never-ending *to-do* lists. Even the best the church can offer is often not enough to get their attention. As the famous and highly regarded philosopher Yogi Berra once said, "If people don't want to come out to the ball park, nobody's gonna stop 'em."[1]

This great observation makes me wonder if there might be some way to take the ball game to them. I believe that in order to most effectively get more fish to swim to your aquarium, you must use both attraction and penetration strategies.

Penetration as a Strategy

Attraction is all about getting *them* to come to us, getting them to meet us on our turf, our terms, and our schedule. Penetration is all about going to them, meeting them on their turf, their terms, and their schedule.

In ancient times, hills were thought of as safe places. In times of war, hills are strategic places. In times of peace, hills are the cherished places. I remember a friend from South Dakota visiting us in California. We were admiring the houses that cling to the hillside overlooking Laguna Beach. He said, "You Californians! You're just crazy for a view." Well, it's not just Californians who love a view from a hilltop.

Jesus used the metaphors of light and a city on a hill.

> You are the light of the world. A city on a hill cannot be hidden. Neither do people light a lamp and put it under a bowl. Instead they put it on its stand, and it gives light to everyone in the house. In the same way, let your light shine before others, that they may see your good deeds and glorify your Father in heaven. (Matthew 5:14-16 TNIV)

This imagery affirms attraction as a strategy. Let your light shine so people can see and be drawn to it. Be a city on the hill, a safe place to which people can come and find safety and hope.

But Jesus also used salt as a metaphor.

> You are the salt of the earth. But if the salt loses its saltiness, how can it be made salty again? It is no longer good for anything, except to be thrown out and trampled underfoot. (Matthew 5:13 TNIV)[2]

Salt in the shaker is of no value. It's not until the salt comes in contact with the food and penetrates it that it's effective.

Salt-shaker churches do not grow. They will not grow until they are turned upside down and shaken out over their communities so the salt can penetrate the lives of family, friends, neighbors, and coworkers.

There are two very practical and strategic reasons why penetration strategies are so important and effective. First, while attraction strategies can be employed by a relative few, effective penetration strategies require broad participation. Nearly every church I assess believes they are the embodiment of Pareto's 80/20 principle. They lament, "Twenty percent of the people do eighty percent of the work." Unfortunately, they are often right. Do you know any successful companies where only a minority of the workers actually works? Why would we expect a church to be effective when only a minority of its people do any work? (The next chapter will deal extensively with the issue of lay involvement.) It makes obvious sense that the more attendees and members there are touching lives in their everyday world, the more the people will be attracted to and retained by the church. The goal should be nothing less than activating every person in your church to "take *it* to them." *It* is the story and presence of Jesus. *It* is the Good News of God's love and Jesus' sacrifice. *It* is their own personal story of God's intervention and involvement in their lives.

The second reason is that people are more responsive when they are met on their turf and on their terms. Thankfully, there is a growing body of resources available to churches that want to be effective with penetration strategies.[3]

The leadership task in this regard is to create a corporate culture, an *ethos* if you please, that makes permeating the community every person's job. The key to success here is to keep it simple and natural. Help people recognize the ordinary, daily opportunities to be good news, which in time create opportunities to speak the Good News. Help people find simple ways to connect with the unchurched and unbelieving. I have seen ordinary people emboldened and empowered by simple sayings like, "Make the front door of your house the side door to your church." Simple hospitality can be a powerfully effective penetration strategy. Remind those who belong to your church that they are part of a team and that it's seldom their responsibility alone to help people into relationship with Jesus and into the life of the church.

For many who lack the gift of evangelism and who are more introverted, inviting people to church is the most effective way for them to invite people to a relationship with Jesus. This presumes, of course, that when their invitees do come with them, they can readily find additional, meaningful relationships; that they will learn why they need a relationship with Jesus and how to enter into that relationship.

This discussion of evangelism by attraction and penetration may at first appear to be a rabbit trail straying from the subject at hand: assimilation. But in reality, effective assimilation begins with expanding the number of visitors you have to retain. So how do you retain a growing percentage of the growing number of visitors?

Getting the Fish to Stay in Your Aquarium

There are three keys to effective retention. They are: an effective assimilation system, meaningful involvement, and relational Velcro®.

According to the dictionary a *system* is "a group of interacting, interrelated, or interdependent elements forming a complex whole."[4] In everyday language, systems consist of numerous interrelated parts all working together, each of which is essential to accomplish a task or outcome. Some elements of an effective assimilation system are:

- Defining *visitor*,[5]
- Defining *assimilated*,

- Creating numerous strategies for gathering personal information from visitors,
- Maintaining an appropriate database to store and retrieve visitor information,
- Recruiting and training people to enter visitor data into the database,
- Developing and implementing a relational and progressive contact strategy to follow up with visitors,
- Distributing reports to the appropriate follow-up channels (people and groups),
- Providing periodic but regular initial entry point events,
- Maintaining numerous effective ongoing entry-point ministries,
- Using the database to track the visitor's progression through the steps to fully assimilated status.[6]

These elements clearly are interacting, interrelated, and interdependent. They form the complex whole called a *system of visitor assimilation*. The more efficient the system, the higher the visitor retention rate.

An effective system always begins with the end in sight. So what is *an assimilated person*? What does it mean to *be assimilated*? Over the years I have seen many churches that consider a person assimilated if he or she is attending worship regularly. Certainly regular worship attendance is a part of an assimilated person's behavior, but it is only a part. Most churches already have an abundant supply of people whose only real involvement is worship attendance. They are not part of small groups. They seldom attend special functions. Church school is not for them. They hold no leadership posts. Many have tried to get them to volunteer, and just as many have failed. I do not know a single church that needs another pew sitter.

What every church can use are more people meaningfully involved in mission and ministry. Churches need more people who are actively helping the church accomplish its mission and vision. It therefore makes sense that an *assimilated* person would be defined as one who not only attends worship regularly but who also participates in a small group and has some meaningful ministry involvement. Indeed, *ministry involvement* is the second key to an effective assimilation system.

The third is *relational Velcro®*. People who want to be alone seldom go where people congregate. When visitors come to church, one or both of two things are usually true. The visitors may have come because a friend invited them. Or they may have come, at least in part, because they want friends and hope to find them there. And, of course, some who come with a friend want to find additional friends. Over the years, numerous research studies have indicated that it takes multiple friendships in the church for a visitor to stay and become an integrated part of the church.

A good assimilation system provides ample opportunity for visitors to meet potential friends in the visitor's first days and weeks at the church. One of the most effective ways of doing this is to create settings where the newcomer meets other newcomers. Long-timers at any church already have numerous significant, often longstanding relationships in the church. They have little capacity for new relationships. While they might add numerous newcomers to their acquaintances they are unlikely to find time to cultivate deep relationships with them.

Most newcomers share something in common. They want friends at the church. Chances are good they will establish some meaningful new friendships if they are around other people seeking meaningful new relationships.

Assimilation is a process. Recognizing the progressive nature of the assimilation process will enhance your church's effectiveness in integrating people into the life of the church. It is helpful to define and track the stages of the process. Establishing criteria for each stage enables you to track a person's progress toward your goal of full assimilation. Let's say you define an assimilated visitor as one who attends worship at least 50 percent of the time, participates in at least one small group, and is involved in at least one form of mission or ministry. You could then create and track three degrees of assimilated status. Meeting any one of the three criteria would constitute being an initially assimilated visitor. Meeting two criteria constitutes a partially assimilated visitor. Meeting all three means that an individual is a fully assimilated visitor and is no longer tracked in your assimilation system.

I am often asked, "What should our retention rate be?" My response is this. The minimum threshold should be 30 percent. If you are not already there, aim at reaching 30 percent. Once you have achieved 30 percent you can strategize for a higher percentage of retained visitors. Ultimately you should strive for a retention rate that exceeds two-thirds (66 percent or more).

CHAPTER FIVE

HOW MANY SERVE?

Ministry involvement is a concept that most church people know. Pastors frequently urge people to "become involved in ministry." Lay leaders and staff members recruit people to teach classes, lead small groups, sing in the choir, play in the praise band, usher, or serve in the nursery. The more programs a church has, the more often its people are called to ministry involvement. No wonder they associate ministry involvement with programs. Since most church programs are conducted on the church campus, people begin to believe that ministry happens at church. Eventually, ministry involvement means, "Come to the church and do something for the church."

After a while, people feel hounded, pressured, and overwhelmed. Some say yes far too often and become overextended. In time they burn out and retreat to the sidelines, letting other people do the work. They say, "I've done my duty," and join the ranks of those who feel that ministry involvement is overemphasized.

Can Mission and Ministry Involvement Be Overemphasized?

As you consider the question, "Can mission and ministry involvement be overemphasized?" you might wonder what mission means. Are *mission* and *ministry* synonymous? You might ask, "Isn't the word *missions*?" *Mission* as it is used here is not synonymous with the word *missions* as most people use it. For most people, *missions* means a few making a career choice, usually going to seminary, becoming a *professional*, leaving family, and going overseas as a missionary. Very few churches overemphasize mission involvement in this sense of the word. As a matter of fact, too many churches are silent on the matter, never challenging their people to consider serving God as a missionary.

Though serving as a professional or career missionary is one way people can be on mission, the words *mission, missions,* and *missionary* are not synonymous. In the context of measuring lay involvement, they are quite distinct. Mission involvement is more about a mind-set than a career. It's not about the few but about everyone. In current books and conversation it's often described as being *missional*.

A *missional* mind-set begins by redefining *vocation*. Most think of their job as their *vocation*. What we get paid for doing is our work and gets priority, for some, the highest priority in life. Our hobbies are our *avocations*. By contrast, people who think missionally believe their *vocation* is "to serve God" and their *avocation* is "whatever they do for a paycheck." Their attitude is that wherever they are and no matter what they are doing, they are "on the mission field," and their purpose is to serve God there. At the office, factory, or store, and in the home or classroom, they are *on mission* for God. Their work on earth is to serve God.

Can mission and ministry involvement be overemphasized? In a word, the answer is no. Mission involvement and the Christian life are inseparable. Being a Christian is to serve God by serving others (Matthew 25:31-46, especially verse 40).

The Key to Personal Spiritual Health

The Mission of Every Believer

Every follower of Jesus shares the same mission. We have a common purpose. How you live out that purpose may look quite different from how another lives it out. His followers fulfilling His purpose for their lives will take varied shapes, colors, and fragrances like an English garden. But the purpose never changes; our mission as His disciples is always the same. So what is that mission?

The apostle Paul declares it in his letter to the church at Ephesus. In his watershed passage clarifying the relationship of grace, faith, and works Paul writes:

> For it is by grace you have been saved, through faith—and this not from yourselves, it is the gift of God—not by works, so that no one can boast. For we are God's workmanship, created in Christ Jesus to do good works, which God prepared in advance for us to do. (Ephesians 2:8-10)

Paul makes it clear that salvation is ours by God's grace. It is not something we earn by doing good things, no matter how many good things we might do. Salvation, the forgiveness of our sins, and a restored relationship with God are gifts God gives. Salvation is not something earned by any good that we do. If it were, it would be payment or a reward and not a gift. The gift of salvation is activated in a person's life by faith. Faith can be defined as taking God at His word and acting on it.

Ephesians 2:8-9 is fundamental to what it means to live a Christian life. Those few words are a real mouthful that Christians have chewed over ever since the days of the early church. In digesting them, people often never get as far as verse 10. "Saved" people—or followers of Jesus— are shaped by God. We are His workmanship and we are created for a single purpose—to do good works!

Christians do not become Christians by doing good works, but we are created to do good works. Doing good works is the purpose of every believer. And here's the most incredible part. God has the good works He intends for us to do in His mind before we are born or become a believer!

If I am a Christian and I am not doing good works, I am not fulfilling the purpose for which He made me. It's even more specific than that. If I am not doing the works He prepared in advance for me to do, I am not living out my God-given purpose as a Christian. Not doing what God has created us to do is to sin. James put it this way, "So then, if you know the good you ought to do and don't do it, you sin" (James 4:17 TNIV).

Peter drove home the same point in a more positive way when he wrote in his first letter, "Live such good lives among the pagans that, though they accuse you of doing wrong, they may see your good deeds and glorify God on the day he visits us" (1 Peter 2:12). When we do the good things He created us to do, we have the great privilege of focusing people on the glory of God. What more important thing could we do with our lives?

In the classic movie *The Blues Brothers*, Elwood and Jake discover that the Saint Helen Orphanage where they were raised cannot make the mortgage payment and is about to be evicted. While attending worship at Triple Rock Church, Jake "sees the light," and they come to believe they are on a mission from God to save the orphanage.

Soon afterward the Blues Brothers are pulled over by a policeman. Elwood is driving. The officer checks his computer and discovers that Elwood's license has been suspended. He has one hundred sixteen outstanding parking warrants and fifty-six moving violations. The computer instructs the officer to "arrest driver . . . impound car."

As the officer asks Elwood to step out of the car, Elwood instead steps on the gas and roars away. The officer calls for backup and gives hot pursuit. Jake says to Elwood, "First you trade the Cadillac for a microphone. Then you lie to me about the band, now you're gonna put me right back in the joint." Elwood responds, "They're not gonna catch us. We're on a mission from God."

Fueled by the conviction that they are on a mission for God, they refuse to be sidetracked or stopped as they pursue their plan to fulfill God's mission. Nothing can stop them. No one can stop them—not the police, the "rednecks," the concert promoters—no one, no way!

I am not suggesting that Jake and Elwood are paragons of Christian maturity, but a key indicator of spiritual life, strength, and health is when Jesus' followers refuses to let anyone or anything hinder them from doing what they believe God has called them to do.

There's More to the Christian Life than Knowing

The Gutenberg press changed the world. It took books from the hands of the elite few and made them readily available to anyone who could read. The advent of the printing press made it possible for people to *see for themselves*, no longer having to rely on the interpretations of professors and priests. The Protestant Reformation was propelled by the printed word. Over time, even common folks had at least a *family* Bible. Today, most Christian households have more Bibles than people.

The ready availability of the Bible has positively impacted individual Christians and churches alike. Familiarity with the Bible and commitment to its authority as God's Word are essential to spiritual vitality.

Timothy's mentor, the apostle Paul, reminded him, "All Scripture is God-breathed and is useful for teaching, rebuking, correcting and training in righteousness, so that all God's people may be thoroughly equipped for every good work" (2 Timothy 3:16-17 TNIV). Through God's Word, He wants to breathe His Truth into our lives. His Truth is useful in shaping us to be increasingly like Him.

No wonder then, that Paul would command Timothy, "Do your best to present yourself to God as one approved, a worker who does not need to be ashamed and who correctly handles the word of truth" (2 Timothy 2:15 TNIV). Bible study is good. It's essential. All Christ followers should feed on a steady diet of not only its "milk" but also its "solid food" (1 Corinthians 3:1-2). In fact the writer of Hebrews spoke quite harshly to those who were not yet digesting the "solid food" of God's Word (Hebrews 5:11-14). People who are not well fed get sick over time. Pictures of malnourished children are so grotesque that most of us can endure only a quick glance or we would be overcome with the horror of starvation. People who are not well fed on the Word of God become spiritually sick over time. People who are not anchored by the Bible drift and run the risk of running aground or striking a sharp rock and sinking.

Studying the Bible and knowing it well are good things. Healthy and effective churches value Bible study, encouraging people to "get into the Word" and to participate in small group Bible studies. High profile, national, international, cross-denominational, community Bible studies can be immensely helpful to individuals and churches alike. Many vibrant churches host such groups.

Without fail, Bible study leading to Bible knowledge will produce health and vitality if the end is kept in mind. Studying the Bible must never be an end in itself. We must never be satisfied with mere Bible knowledge, no matter how expansive it might be. Let's return for a moment to that seminal text about the Bible, 2 Timothy 3:16-17. The Bible can be used to teach, rebuke, correct, and train. In that way it is useful in our lives. But useful to what end, useful for what purpose? Look at verse 17 again, ". . . so that all God's people may be thoroughly equipped for every good work." In other words, there is more to the Christian life than mere knowing.

I love the words of that eminent "theologian," Mark Twain, who said, "It ain't those parts of the Bible that I can't understand that bother me, it is the parts that I do understand."[1] Twain grasped the reality that the Christian life is not only about knowing; it is also about doing. It's important to remember that *the doing* is not the doing of *religious things* but rather the doing of "good works" (Ephesians 2:10; James 2:17-18). Putting it succinctly, every follower of Jesus has been commissioned and called to ministry. An uninvolved Christian is an unhealthy Christian.

Which Comes First, the Knowing or the Doing?

Both individuals and institutions take the shape of the culture in which they live. It takes intentional and concerted effort to resist the shape of the culture and remain true to God's intended shape that transcends culture. When it comes to teaching and learning, many churches in America act as though learning best happens in a classroom, with a teacher lecturing through a curriculum while students fill notebooks and pass tests. After you finish your studies and get your degree, then you are ready to apply your knowledge in the real world. Everyone has experienced the limitations of this philosophy. Who among us does not know at least one person who has more education than he or she knows how to use? They do not or cannot apply what they *know* to the real world. We often dismiss them by saying, "They are too educated for their own good." It's the *summa cum laude* MBA graduate who cannot manage. It's the professor whose only real world experience ended in failure. It's the pastor with the doctorate who cannot lead or preach a sermon anyone can understand. It's the Christian who has been through five different evangelism-training programs who cannot walk someone over the bridge to faith in Jesus.

When I was a young pastor, a friend and I managed to arrange breakfast alone with a world-renowned preacher. We valued preaching highly, and we were excited at the prospect of picking the brain of this master communicator over bacon and eggs. Our third question of the morning was met with a surprising response. "Boys," the preacher said, "don't ask me too many questions about what I'm doing when I preach. Fact is I do not know what I'm doing. I just do it." He went on to say he had recently been offered the Preaching Chair at what he termed "a prestigious seminary." After some thought and, presumably, prayer he told them, "I will come to your seminary and preach, and you can tell me what I am doing." He told us his story. In England where he was raised they believed in the "sink or swim" theory of learning. You are taught to swim by being thrown in the lake. When he was still a young teenager, a church leader approached him and told him it was time for him to learn to preach and that he was to preach on a certain Sunday evening in about two or three weeks.

No doubt he knew a lot more about preaching than he was letting on. I suspect he did not want his breakfast interrupted with a lot of thinking and talking about preaching, and this was his kind way of telling a couple of eager young preacher wannabes to give him some space. But the fact is he learned to preach by preaching, and he learned what he knew about preaching later on in the doing. In some instances, maybe even most instances, the best learning happens simultaneously with the doing.

The Key to Corporate Spiritual Health

Healthy, growing churches infuse their members with the idea they are all on a mission from God. Decades ago I saw a pastor's business card. I still remember it, so it obviously made an impression. The card had the usual information—name of church, address, and phone number. What made the card memorable was this. In the lower left corner was the word "Pastor," followed by the pastor's name. In the lower right corner the word "Ministers" was followed by "All of the People" I have no idea how many of the people understood they were the ones doing ministry at their church, but the fact that their pastor understood greatly increased the probability that many of them did, too.

The Importance of Keeping People Busy

There are numerous reasons why lay involvement is crucial to the corporate health of a church, but I want to highlight two. The first reason relates to the importance of keeping them busy—busy doing the right things.

The principle is this. If being on a mission from God does not occupy them, people will find their own preoccupations. Furthermore, you can count on this; their preoccupations will seldom help the church accomplish the mission God has given it. They will become preoccupied with things of no real significance. Have you ever sat through a two-hour board meeting while people discussed whether or not the women's missionary circle should be allowed to padlock the cupboard with *their* supplies inside? I once consulted with a church whose trustees let bees live in the ceiling and drip honey on the platform for years because the men could not decide on the best way to resolve the problem. Despite my years of consulting with churches, I am still amazed at how often people will squabble over things that just don't matter.

Keep them busy doing the right things or they will drive you and each other nuts over the silliest of things. The right things are those that help the church accomplish its mission and vision. Help people identify the specific tasks to which God has called them. Help them identify their spiritual gifts and create settings in which they can make use of them.

The Power of Simple Numbers

A second reason why lay involvement is crucial to the corporate health of the church has to do with simple numbers. It goes like this: two can usually do more than one, four can usually do more than two, eight can usually do more than four, and so on. Like I said, "Simple numbers."

The more lay people involved in ministry, the more a church will accomplish. There is a strong correlation between the number of people mobilized in ministry and the effectiveness of the church. The more people who invite family, friends, neighbors, and coworkers to church, the more visitors a church will see. The more teachers who teach others to teach while teaching their classes, the more teachers a church will have and the better it will be able to deal with growth.

Have you ever wondered why the American church—with all its advantages, freedom, and wealth—cannot keep up with population growth, while house churches in places like China and Vietnam are growing exponentially? Most of our churches have facilities (sometimes huge facilities on many acres), degreed pastors (sometimes larger staffs than many house churches have members), experienced lay leaders, and ample money (in spite of what we think). Our churches are heavily populated with people who have studied the Bible for most of their lifetime. Most churches in China and Vietnam are poor and are led by pastors who have no formal training and no seminary degrees. They lack trained lay leaders and have no permanent church facilities. People who came to believe in Jesus within the past three to six months or sometimes just three to six weeks are often the pastors in their churches. Why are they growing so rapidly while we can't keep up with population growth?

In large measure it's about simple numbers. Our church pews are filled with far too many people who attend worship on Sunday, leave, and return some time within the next two or three weeks to attend worship, leave, and return to hear a special speaker at a potluck and then leave only to return again in about two or three weeks for worship. In global churches, all members understand they are on mission. They learn so they can be effective on mission. They understand that each one is expected to bring others into the church and to faith in Jesus. If the house church consists of twenty-five, there will typically be twenty or more who are actively involved in mission and ministry. And their churches grow!

Some years ago a bright and deeply committed young businessman engaged me in conversation. He learned of my long-standing involvement in Vietnam. He asked many questions about the humanitarian work we do. He asked almost as many questions about the state of the church in Vietnam. He was a member of Saddleback Church in Lake Forest, California, and believed strongly in the purpose-driven model. Finally he asked me, "Are there any purpose-driven churches in Vietnam?" I responded, "Absolutely! In Vietnam they are all purpose-driven churches."

He knew I meant something other than what he had just asked and said, "What do you mean?" I said, "If you can lose your relationship with your family, lose your job, suffer persecution, maybe even lose your freedom, or in rare instances lose your life, you do church on purpose. House church members clearly understand the purpose of their churches. The purpose of their church is to win as many people to Jesus Christ as possible, and they understand they have a responsibility to help that happen. As individuals and as churches they are clearly purpose-driven."

Wherever the church is located, for the sake of both believer and church, church leaders must call all to ministry involvement. They must count and know how many are serving. The percentage of those serving is a measure of the leaders' effectiveness. Mobilizing the laity is not optional; it's a mandate. It is a leader's task to make mission and ministry involvement normative. Leaders must have high expectations for ministry involvement on the part of their people.

Measuring the Full Scope of Ministry Involvement

How do you measure ministry involvement? How can you measure the degree to which the lay people in your church are mobilized? In order to capture the full scope of ministry involvement, you must take into account three arenas of involvement.

Involving People in the Church

The most obvious and common measure of lay involvement is to measure the number of people involved in serving on campus in the ministries and programs of the church. How many teach Sunday school or lead a Bible study? How many are involved in the music and worship ministry? How many serve on boards, committees, or ministry teams? Are they involved in children's ministries, leading the men's ministry, or working with the youth program?

Each church will define for itself what constitutes ministry involvement. The regular weekly or monthly involvements obviously qualify. If someone ushers once a month, will you count that as "involved in ministry"? If a long-time attendee does nothing but participate in a three-day Christmas pageant in December, does that constitute involved? Perhaps you will create categories of involvement with ministries like teaching, program leadership, and worship team involvement considered A-level with service in one such capacity constituting *involved*. The second category, B-level, might consist of sporadic, less demanding roles with two or more such involvements constituting *involved*. Almost every church I work with has an animated discussion about what *gets credit* and what doesn't. My experience is that church personalities and cultures differ so much that each must come to its own list.

Keep it simple. Maybe the two-tiered approach is already too complicated for you. Making your system of counting more complicated than the two-tiered or some other similar approach will not significantly improve the accuracy of your measurement, and the complexity of it will likely militate against staying with it. It works if you simply list the ministry or service roles that constitute the level of service involvement you want to see in your people and credit only those things as involvement.[2]

An added benefit of tracking people's involvement in the church is that you can tell quickly not only who is not involved in service but also who is over-extended. Tracking this data can help you coach people away from church involvement at the expense of their family or their ability to be a witness in their community.

Involving People in the Community

Most churches give people *credit* for serving if a person is involved in some ministry in the church and on campus. Some pastors and lay leaders subtly make their people feel guilty if they choose to be involved in the community rather than the church. But a high percentage of people involved in serving the community can be an accurate indicator of a church's health and effectiveness.

Becoming a "Favored" Church

One of the most interesting insights into the life of the early church is found in Acts 2.

> Every day they continued to meet together in the temple courts. They broke bread in their homes and ate together with glad and sincere hearts, praising God and enjoying the favor of all the people. And the Lord added to their number daily those who were being saved. (Acts 2:46-47)

The early church "enjoyed the favor of all the people"! No way can that be said of most churches today. The unchurched, unbelieving community frequently views the church with disdain, seeing it as a *scold*, filled with hypocrites who tell others how to live when their own lives are less than exemplary. How did the church lose favor with the community? It may be that we went from *doing* to *talking* and *telling*. Author Brennan Manning might be on target with his suggestion that today's church should "return to the discipline of the secret."[3] Manning points us in the direction of less talk and more action, specifically more service to the community, more acts of mercy and justice.

As I survey the church landscape in the United States today, I am encouraged by the number of churches that are reawakening to the importance of community involvement. Milfred Minatrea's book *Shaped by God's Heart* (Jossey-Bass, 2004) tells of numerous churches that are finding favor by serving their communities. Rick Rusaw and Eric Swanson write of similar churches in their book *The Externally Focused Church* (Group Publishers, 2004). Both books are profoundly helpful for churches that want to be the hands and feet of Jesus in their communities. Each contains stories of churches that are *telling* by their *doing*. They point us to churches that have found favor in their communities. Your church could join their ranks.

Deploying People in the Community

Truth is, most churches already have people serving God in the community. They often serve quietly, out of the eye of church leaders. Wise pastors and lay leaders find them and honor them, celebrating their ministries and making them heroes of the congregation. So counting the people who serve in the community begins by systematically surveying your people to discover those who already have a community-based ministry.

The shape of their ministries is endless. They volunteer as teacher's aides, tutors; serve as hospital volunteers, coaches, Big Sisters, community senior center leaders, and drivers for the elderly and persons with disabilities. They supervise after-school programs, visit shut-ins, give hospice care, keep records at the local free health clinic, and raise money for the American Cancer Society.

In addition to counting them and giving them equal *credit* with those who serve in the church, church leaders have another task to do. They must ensure that these people know how to do their service in Jesus' name. These volunteers often need help in making their service to others also serve God. The hospital will train them to be hospital volunteers. Only the church can teach them to be Christian hospital volunteers, making their service count not only in time but also for eternity. Help them know how to do the good works God has in mind for them to do.

Pastors and lay leaders do well when they discover and resource those who are already active in serving the community. They do even better when they encourage others to serve God in the community. Wise leaders of highly effective churches are regularly identifying, recruiting, and training people, helping them find places of service in their neighborhoods and communities. Wise leaders know how many community servants there are and where they are serving.[4]

Involving People throughout the World

The third arena for involvement in mission and ministry is what I call "serving in the world." The most obvious expression of this type of service is to be a pastor or career missionary.

A Better Way

It is a good thing when churches support career missionaries with prayer and money. It is an indirect way of involving people in ministry throughout the world. But is there an even better way? How about helping those who are a part of your church hear God's call and follow Him in obedience to serve needy people somewhere in the world. How about knowing you had a hand in their finding a place of service as you pray for them and write that check to help support them?[5]

Imagine the satisfaction of knowing that God is using people in pastoral ministry because you and your church encouraged them to serve God in that context. No pastor ever had a more profound influence in my life than Bob Paulson. While I was in high school, God used Pastor Paulson to bring me to a warm, personal relationship with Jesus. On a vacation during my first year in seminary, I spent an evening telling Pastor Paulson all the reasons I was not going to finish seminary and why I would never serve as a parish pastor. He listened intently. He asked a few questions, mostly clarifying questions. He did not argue with me. He did not preach.

The next morning he said, "Bill, I have been thinking about last night. I understand all your reasons. Most of them make sense to me. But I want you to remember just one thing. Remember, Bill, we need guys like you in the ministry." I dismissed his comment as a kind thing said by a pastor who liked me and wanted to compliment me. But for the next two and a half years, whenever it was quiet and my mind was not otherwise occupied, I would hear Bob Paulson's voice saying, "Remember, Bill, we need guys like you in the ministry." One day I realized it was not Bob Paulson's voice I had been hearing; it was God's voice calling me to ministry.

Until his death some years later, I know Pastor Paulson watched me with satisfaction. He delighted in knowing I was where I was and that God was using me, in part because of his influence. I am not the only one. There are about a dozen of us who have spent our entire adult lives serving as pastors and missionaries because Bob Paulson was determined to involve people in serving God in the world.

A Different Way

Steering people into pastoral or missionary service is not the only way a church can deploy people throughout the world. A church can make an even greater impact by helping people learn to serve Jesus first and make a living second or, put another way, helping them learn how to serve Jesus as they make a living.

A Christian businesswoman in Vietnam understood this concept. As she launched her company, she first hired Christians in order to help them make a fair living wage. But more than that she was creating a Christian atmosphere in her company. As her business grew, she began hiring Buddhists. As the Buddhists worked among Christians, they began to inquire about Christianity. Over time, many of them became Christians. Part of the owner's business plan was to use her company as a setting for evangelism. She illustrates what it means to *serve in the world*.

What if your church became intentional about placing people in ministry throughout the world? What might happen if you began planting the idea that a business owner could open a branch of his or her company in another country so that he or she could be a tentmaker missionary to that country?[6] What if the country were a controlled one, like China or Vietnam, where career missionaries are not welcome? Is it possible that in three to five years your church might see some of its people becoming involved in ministry throughout the world? Could it be that your church should set a goal to commission a certain number of career and vocational missionaries from your church over the next five to ten years?

Recently, while consulting with St. John's, a large Lutheran church in Southern California,[7] the staff and lay leaders began chewing on this idea. They wondered how to define the word *missionary*. What about the man in their church who started a business to provide after-school tutoring to language-bound first generation Hispanic students throughout the county? It is a business, but he treats it like a ministry. Through staffing and curriculum, spiritual values permeate the tutoring centers. Students often find faith and find their way to church through his business. Does he count as a person involved in the world? We know he is not a career missionary sent by a mission board, but is he a vocational missionary?

St. John's chose to define *missionary* as "anyone who ministers to those who cannot or will not come to our church." Thinking this way helps them be highly effective in involving their people in mission and ministry in both the community and the world. A similar mind-set could make a huge difference in your church's effectiveness.

CHAPTER SIX

WHO ARE YOUR NEW LEADERS?

In assessing churches we typically ask the leaders, "When was your church's 'golden era'?" We tell them *now* is an acceptable answer. All too often they cite a period in the past. Occasionally they point to a past era but indicate they are now in what they consider a second golden era. Why do we find so many peaks and valleys of health and effectiveness in so many churches, especially those with long histories?

We all know churches that flourished for a season. They grew in size, reputation, and influence. Some flourished long enough to become legendary. People studied them, wrote about them, envied them, and flocked to them in order to learn "how it should be done." Time passed, and these vibrant churches lost their luster. They plateaued. They declined. Eventually, they became a shadow of their former self. The large, once-crowded sanctuary now hosts a handful of people for one service on Sunday mornings. Silence fills empty classrooms, hallways, and meeting areas for days and weeks on end.

How does this happen? Why does it happen so often? While each church's story might have some unique aspects, and while there often are numerous contributing factors, there is always one underlying, fundamental, common cause to the demise of once-great churches. They failed to raise up new leaders.

Why Do So Few Churches Sustain Health and Effectiveness Long-term?

A church with peaks and valleys in its ministry effectiveness will discover that the peaks and valleys coincide with the quality of leaders resident in the church over its history. In some churches, the peaks frequently coincide with a certain pastor's tenure. Decades later people will wistfully say, "Ah yes, those were the Dr. Thompson years."

In an assessment done some years ago, we discovered the current pastor was severely hampered in his leadership because the shadow of his predecessor twice removed still cast a dark pall over the church. The pastor during the church's golden years had died physically but was still very much alive in the minds of many long-timers. The very first words of my assessment report were, "Dr. Wells is dead." Dr. Wells had failed to raise up highly competent leaders to follow him. The church predictably declined and was in a deepening valley. If it was ever to experience another golden era, it needed to give its current, highly gifted pastor the freedom to lead in new ways to new places. The lesson to be learned is this: that church did not extend its years of peak ministry effectiveness because Dr. Wells had not raised up leaders as good as or even better than he was.

In some churches, the peaks coincide with the presence of a key lay leader, a gifted and benign "church boss" who had the church's best interests at heart. His or her steady hand, inherent wisdom, and leadership skills allowed the church to enjoy a prolonged period of ministry effectiveness. Typically, the passing of this key leader marks the beginning of a valley for the church. Same problem. The lay leader failed to raise up new leaders to succeed him or her. The leader's passing through failing health, moving, or death creates a leadership vacuum, and the church suffers.

Different scenarios, same underlying problem: effective leaders did not identify, recruit, and train new leaders to take their place.

Practicing an Opportunistic Approach to Leadership

Most churches rely upon chance to provide the quality leaders they need. As a young pastor in a rapidly growing church, I remember praying, "Lord, send some seasoned leaders from other churches among the many new people you are bringing here." The church's growth was outstripping our current supply of leaders. Most of our growth was new Christians coming from unchurched backgrounds. I prayed as I did because I had not yet learned the fundamental rule of church leadership: "Grow your own!"

The opportunistic approach to leadership suffers from many deficiencies. There are not that many good leaders in other churches. Most churches long for more and better leaders. The pool of ready-made outstanding leaders is not well stocked. The reasons leaders move to new churches vary. Sometimes the reasons are legitimate. They have moved and are looking for a new place to serve. But sometimes they have left that other church because of conflict with the pastor or other leaders. Maybe they suddenly *become available* in your church because they did inappropriate things in their former church and had to leave. Every leader from another church comes with his or her own vision of church and preferred ways of leading based on his or her experience in other churches. New leaders must be acculturated to your church—its vision, its ethos, its ways of doing things. Sometimes they do not absorb these things, and their presence becomes divisive. The problem with the opportunistic approach to filling leadership needs is that it leaves too much to mere chance.

Overlooking the Importance of Leadership

A common denominator in all highly effective churches is excellent leadership. That leadership may come from a gifted, charismatic pastor. It may be found in a key lay leader or two. In the best of circumstances, numerous outstanding leaders populate a church's leadership community.[1] The writer of Proverbs said it this way, "Without wise leadership, a nation falls; / there is safety in having many advisers" (Proverbs 11:14 NLT).

Most give lip service to the importance of leadership. There are phrases commonly cited by a wide variety of people. Mary Kay Ash, businesswoman and entrepreneur, frequently told her sales directors, "The speed of the leader is the speed of the gang." Erskine Bowles, businessman and former White House Chief of Staff, declared his conviction that "leadership is the key to 99 percent of all successful efforts."[2]

If leadership is so crucial, why do we leave it to chance, at worst, or presume upon God's intervention, at best? Shortsightedness might cause some churches to ignore the need for intentional, systematic leadership development. The thinking goes like this: "Things are going great, and our current leaders are outstanding and deeply committed. We don't need to develop more leaders."

Some leaders do not raise up new leaders because of pride. They honestly believe no one can do it as well as they can. Their mantras are: "It's easier to do it myself," and "If you want it done right, you have to do it yourself." Still other leaders do not raise up new leaders because of ego needs that are met in the leadership position they hold. Fear of losing or having to share the power, prestige, and prominence that go with being the pastor or a key leader in a church keeps some from preparing others to lead. There are other reasons leaders fail to raise up new leaders. None are valid. None are in the best interest of the church. None are pleasing to God.

Over the years, my experience has increasingly convinced me that the primary task of a leader is to produce more leaders. Conventional wisdom says that a leader's primary task is to lead well. Like you, I have observed countless leaders whose church, ministry, or company thrived under their leadership only to decline, or even crash and burn, after they left. Rather than good leaders I consider them to be good managers. They managed well and their organization did well while they were at the helm. But they failed to look ahead. They failed to anticipate a future after themselves. True leaders do not live solely in the here and now. Leaders are out in front, ahead of others. They read the future landscape and think long before others about what it will take to succeed in that future. If they ignored the task of shaping others to lead, they managed well but failed to lead.

A quotation widely attrbiuted to Ralph Nader captures the heart of the issue, "I start with the premise that the function of leadership is to produce more leaders, not more followers." Harvey S. Firestone, the American industrialist and founder of the Firestone Tire and Rubber Company, is reported to have put it this way, "The growth and development of people is the highest calling of leadership." The apostle Paul instructed Timothy to produce more leaders when he said, "And the things you have heard me say in the presence of many witnesses entrust to reliable people who will also be qualified to teach others" (2 Timothy 2:2 TNIV). Jesus invested Himself in a dozen to whom He ultimately trusted the future of His church.

Creating a System for Leader Development

Long-term productivity in churches requires the continual development of effective new leaders. The absence of a system for leader development constitutes the primary organizational barrier to long-term effectiveness and growth. Creating and utilizing a system to develop leaders removes the barrier and clears the way for a long period of peak ministry effectiveness.

Churches that effectively develop their own ongoing supply of leaders never depend on one, two, or even a few leaders to develop more leaders. They have a system for developing leaders. This system looks different from church to church. But all good leader development systems have four essential elements. They all *identify, recruit, train,* and *deploy* leaders. Little is left to chance. Leaders are often prepared before the need is apparent.

Identify Potential Leaders

Any good system for developing leaders begins with identifying potential leaders. The entrance process, by which new people become assimilated into the life of the church, can be used to discover those who might have leadership potential. It's not uncommon for churches to use this vehicle to discover ministry workers. It's relatively simple and is a good strategy to begin the search for new leaders in this setting.

As you seek to identify potential new leaders, remember that the best indicator of future effectiveness is past performance. If someone has effectively led one ministry, program, or organization he or she will typically be effective in leading another.

If a person does not have a leadership track record, help them create one. Find a ministry role for them. Give them the training and authority necessary for them to succeed. Coach them. Observe them. If they do well in that role, move them to a more substantial leadership role. Over time they will demonstrate their leadership abilities, character qualities, and spiritual maturity—all of which are key aspects of quality leaders.[3]

Jim Collins, author of *Good to Great* (HarperCollins, 2001), offers a helpful grid with his concept of five levels of leadership.[4] The five levels are a progression of leadership skills that begins with being a highly capable individual, then a contributing team member, a competent manager, an effective leader, and finally a Level 5 leader who is an executive leader.

His levels, labels, and their definitions are helpful. But perhaps most helpful is his reminder that being a leader is not a *nirvana*-like state of maturity or perfection that only a few somehow magically attain; it is a progression of leadership stages through which one can progress over time. At any given time a church needs leaders at all levels of development.

Recruit Potential Leaders

The Usual Way

Most churches recruit on the basis of institutional need. A worker or leader is needed for one of the church's programs. The recruiters do a mental review of the people they know and identifies someone who could fill the spot. The thought process or discussion goes like this. "They teach school, so they could certainly teach fourth grade boys." "They have an accounting firm, don't they? They'd be good on the finance committee." "They're already involved in two ministries, but this will only take a couple of hours a week. Hey, when you want something done, always ask a busy person!" The pastor, staff member, or key lay leader who is most likely to succeed at convincing them is sent to talk them into filling the open slot.

In some instances, by God's grace, people are recruited to places where they experience effectiveness, find fulfillment, and remain for a significant time. But in far too many instances, people agree to serve in the wrong role for the wrong reasons. Too often they are not effective. They find it an unrewarding chore and burn out, becoming mere pew sitters who have "done their turn."

My favorite example of institutional recruiting happened in a church in Minnesota. One Sunday morning the second grade Sunday school class marched onto the platform and sang two songs as part of the worship service. Parents beamed, grandparents sat proudly, and the hearts of the congregation melted. The entire congregation smiled while the children were herded off the platform and back to their classroom. The pastor stood and announced, "We have been trying to recruit a new teacher for these beautiful children for over two months, with no success. If one of you does not step forward this week to volunteer to be their teacher, there will not be a class for these second graders next Sunday."

If you are thinking of copying this page so you can pass it on to your children's ministries recruiter, you need to hear the rest of the story. A tender heart in the congregation could not bear the thought of these adorable children without a class for want of a teacher and called the church office late in the week. Learning no one else had stepped forward, she volunteered. She could not tell a story well enough to keep the children's attention and no amount of training seemed to help her. She had long forgotten that second graders do not sit still for an hour and often start talking, sometimes loudly, when others are already talking. They were a lot cuter when lined up on the platform singing than when running loose in a classroom. It was a disaster. She was relieved of her duty. She was relieved to be relieved, but her pride was hurt and she never took another ministry assignment.

The Sunday school needed a teacher and recruited one in a most institutional manner. You've likely seen it done in your church. Maybe it's been done to you! And you have thought, "There must be a better way."

A Better Way

There is a better way, a recruitment system built on matching a person's skills, spiritual gifts, passions, and sense of call with a ministry role. An effective system of leader recruitment begins with a comprehensive and repeated means of helping people identify their skills and spiritual gifts.[5]

In the assessment process, we often hear a leader say, "We did a spiritual gifts inventory, let's see, maybe five years ago." Often in the very same church we hear someone lament saying, "I took some gifts test and I wrote down jobs I would be willing to do but I have not heard a word from anyone in over two years." Obviously no one shared with the person the gifts identified by the inventory. The information is likely sitting dormant on the computer hard drive of someone who may not even know they have it. No one extended the courtesy of even responding to their offer to serve, much less help them find a meaningful place of service.

The better way of recruiting takes more than gifts and skills into account. Leaders will spend time with potential leaders to discover what they are passionate about. What do they really *want* to do? What is in their heart? What must they do or die? The apostle Paul's passion was preaching. He said, "Yet when I preach the gospel, I cannot boast, for I am compelled to preach. Woe to me if I do not preach the gospel" (1 Corinthians 9:16-17)! Wise leaders spend enough time with people to discover their "Woe to me if I do not..."

The better way also takes their sense of God's call into account. What do people believe God has called them to do? God's call is not only on missionaries and the professional clergy. God calls all believers to serve Him. In Acts, Jesus clearly affirmed His universal call on all His followers: "But you will receive power when the Holy Spirit comes on you; and you will be my witnesses in Jerusalem, and in all Judea and Samaria, and to the ends of the earth" (Acts 1:8). Peter wrote about this call in his first letter saying, "Each one should use whatever gift he has received to serve others, faithfully administering God's grace in its various forms" (1 Peter 4:10-11 TNIV).

When people are doing what God has called them to do, they will be passionate about it. When people are serving God with passion and a sense of God's calling, they are doing what God made them to do. They will not burn out. They will be fruitful, and they will not be diminished in the effort. Parker Palmer, the Quaker teacher and author, makes this point by quoting from May Sarton's poem "Now I Become Myself." She writes of the fruit tree that from its barren winter branches grows leaves, then blossoms, and finally, fruit. The fruit ripens and eventually drops to the ground but "does not exhaust the root." The root of the tree is not diminished by all this effort, because it is simply doing what God created it to do.[6]

A good leader development system annually assesses the spiritual gifts not only of new people but also of all in the church. A good system meets with those assessed and shares with them the results of the gift inventory. Such a system discerns each person's passions and sense of call. In a good system leaders and potential leaders talk periodically, seeing if there is a match with some ministry opportunity. Those periodic conversations also consider the person's passion and sense of God's call as ministry opportunities are reviewed.

Train the Recruited

Author Anthony Jay is reported to argue, "The only real training for leadership is leadership."[7] Russ Bredholt, a respected leader, strategist, and consultant, would agree. In a 2005 interview for *Private Clubs Magazine Online*, he said,

> Seventy percent of leadership development is getting the right kind of experience. Morgan McCall, an author and professor of management at the University of Southern California, has identified five things that contribute to one's growth: starting something from scratch; fixing or

turning something around; enlarging your responsibility; task assignments; and hardships.[8]

The best leader training systems seldom start with classes or even reading. The starting point is the real world of real ministry with a supervisor functioning as teacher, mentor, and coach. Classes and books augment the learning already begun in the swift current of ministry leadership. Frequent exposure to successful practitioner-leaders and best practice churches helps people *see* how it is done.

The supervisor role is central in effective leader training systems. Leaders are never left alone to grow. Training is anything but hands-off and *laissez-faire*. Supervisors may be given a variety of names, but their function is always the same. *Supervisor* is a good term since it speaks of a direct, frequent, supportive, and accountable relationship. The supervisor's task is to develop leaders by coaching and equipping them for success in the trainees' current leadership role.[9]

Deploy Trained Leaders

By now it is obvious to you. The best leader development systems are neither linear nor sequential. The emphasis may change, but in the real world identification, recruitment, training, and deployment are concurrent and continual.

Listen to pastors and lay leaders talk about developing leaders. They will speak of training a person to be an elder or a teacher or a small group leader. They are training people to fill roles and manage ministries. This mind-set is more institutional than organic. It is linear and sequential.

A better mind-set recognizes that identifying the potential in a leader often happens when the person is already deployed in a leadership role. That leader (we'll call him or her Leader One) is recruited to a different, more demanding, and more strategic leadership role and is deployed in that position. Training happens on the job under the tutelage of a supervisor who coaches, mentors, equips, and holds him or her accountable. Leader One in turn becomes supervisor to Leader Two, helping him or her become capable of assuming Leader One's role. As the process unfolds, Leader One may be identified as a potential leader for a still different role, and the process is repeated.

Such a system is more cyclical than linear; it is more process-driven than task-driven, where the task is to fill the vacant position. A cyclical or organic system produces more leaders because it practices reproduction. It produces leaders who lead from a wide and varied experience base rather than the tunnel vision of one who has only been treasurer for twenty years. This kind of holistic system creates a fluidity among leaders that counteracts the institutional tendency for leadership structures to calcify and be filled with fossilized *long-termers*. The more a church reflects this kind of leader development system, the longer it will sustain ministry effectiveness.[10]

Measuring Your Effectiveness in Developing Leaders

The actual metrics involved in measuring your church's effectiveness in developing leaders is infinitely easier than the task itself. You simply count the number of new people who have been identified, recruited, trained, and deployed during the time frame being evaluated.[11] How many people are now at some level of ministry leadership role who were not leading on any of Jim Collins's five levels a year ago?

To measure, you must agree upon a definition of a *new leader*. You might define a *new leader* as a person currently in a leadership role who was not in any kind of leadership role in your church one year ago.

Further you must define *ministry role*. You should include both ministry or program roles, and governance roles. Too many churches tacitly define leadership roles as governance or management roles such as board member, committee member, or church officer (church chair or financial secretary). In the real scheme of things, the more important leaders are the church's ministry leaders. Churches do well when they recruit their best and brightest to serve in ministry leadership rather than sit on boards and committees.

Churches demonstrate great wisdom when they create an ethos where ministry leaders are given greater honor than those who serve in governance roles. Those who govern the church are the servants of the church; their primary role is to provide for and support those who are doing the ministry of the church.

Generally speaking, effectiveness is enhanced when a church limits its governance positions to a handful and continually expands the number of ministry leaders. The relative health and effectiveness of a church can be measured by the ratio of ministry leaders to governance leaders. The higher the ratio of ministry leaders to governance leaders, the more effective the church will be. Therefore you might wish to calculate the ratio of ministry leaders to governance leaders.

It is quite helpful to break your count down into Jim Collins's five levels, noting how many new leaders are in each phase of development. Large churches may want to establish goals in each of the five levels, but for most churches, setting one goal (raising up new leaders encompassing all five levels) proves sufficient.

DO YOU REALLY GROW BY STAYING SMALL?

y voice is but one in a large chorus, all singing the same tune, "Small groups are essential to the health and growth of churches." In more than three decades of observing churches and two decades of church consulting, I cannot recall a healthy, growing congregation where a significant small group ministry was not present.

It might seem counterintuitive, but the path to becoming large is by staying small. In the world of church growth, we often hear of barriers to growth. The first, most common church growth hurdle is the famous *200 barrier*. Fundamentally, two factors contribute to the *200 barrier*. The first is leadership—the pastor's and/or board's inability or unwillingness to change their leadership style or the church's leadership structures. The second contributing factor is small groups, or more specifically, the lack of them.

Small churches function like small groups. Everyone knows everyone else. If people miss, their absence is noticed, and at least one person will check up to find out why they weren't there. The small group leader (the pastor) can function as chaplain to all and provide personal, direct care to those in need of spiritual or emotional attention. It's relatively easy for all to be in on the news, so communication is uncomplicated. People know why the church exists (usually for them and their needs), and they know the rules (what's permissible and what is not).

Arguably a church of up to one hundred seventy or one hundred eighty in attendance is, by definition, a small group. One key reason for the existence of the *200 barrier* is that beyond two hundred, the church can no longer function as a small group and must develop a network of small groups. Its existing informal small groups must be transitioned into small groups with both community and missional purposes. Transitioning from a single-cell to a multi-cell church is not automatic. It never happens *naturally*. It takes intentionality and strategic action on the part of leaders, and if leaders do not lead in this regard, the church will never grow significantly beyond the two hundred mark.

The *200 barrier* is real, so real that many at the forefront of church planting utilize "large birth weight" strategies in order to help churches pass the *200 barrier* by never having to experience it. If the church exceeds two hundred at its launch, it will never have to figure out how to move from being a single-cell to a multi-cell church. It will, of necessity, be a multi-cell church from the outset.

Continued and sustained growth far beyond the two hundred mark requires a robust small group life. If a church of any size fails to nurture and emphasize its small group life, its growth will be slowed. If that church fails to reenergize its small groups, it will not only cease to grow but will begin to decline. A universally common factor in the decline of once growing churches is the deterioration of small groups. Yes, you do grow larger by staying small.

Can Something so *Yesterday* Be so Crucial for *Tomorrow?*

I am sometimes amused when reading today's small group champions. Some talk about small groups as though small groups in church life are something new. Recently I read of one leader who stated that the church's "discovery" of small groups could be traced back to the ministry of Lyman Coleman and the Navigators *way back in the early 1970s!* The Western church today is not discovering small groups. At best we are *rediscovering* something that is as old as God and core to our very being as Christians and churches.

Where did small groups go that they needed to be rediscovered with the help of Lyman Coleman and others in the late twentieth century? How can there be so many churches that today, in the beginning of the twenty-first century, do not understand the importance of small groups?

A Brief Historical Perspective on Small Groups

Small Groups Are as Old as God

Weird as it may sound, could it be possible that small groups began with God? According to the Bible, the One God is Three. Wise scholars throughout the centuries have attempted to explain that contradictory truth. Now I have no delusions of being the one to unlock the mystery of the Trinity. I hold loosely all that I think I know about the Trinity. But I do have some thoughts about the three-in-one God we worship and serve. One such thought is that God might well be the first and the ultimate small group.

> Then God said, "Let us make human beings in our image, in our likeness, so that they may rule over the fish in the sea and the birds in the sky, over the livestock and all the wild animals, and over all the creatures that move along the ground."
>
> So God created human beings in his own image, in the image of God he created them; male and female he created them. (Genesis 1:26-27 TNIV)

For me, the Genesis passage conjures up a mental image of God the Father, Son, and Holy Spirit meeting together as an architectural design group discussing and deciding the shape and purpose of humankind. When all members of the group were in agreement, the One God acted and created humans as the architectural design group had agreed. Furthermore, He made humans "in his own image," which would mean that somehow, in some way, small group life is at the core of all of us.

Small Groups Are Thoroughly Biblical

The writer of Ecclesiastes taught a profound small group principle in an elegantly simple manner.

> Two are better than one,
> because they have a good return for their labor:
>
> If they fall down,
> they can help each other up.
> But pity those who fall
> and have no one to help them up!

73

> Also, if two lie down together, they will keep warm.   .
>   But how can one keep warm alone?
>
> Though one may be overpowered,
>   two can defend themselves.
> A cord of three strands is not quickly broken.
> (Ecclesiastes 4:9-12 TNIV)

Jesus indicated that prayer was not to be limited to solitary conversations between one person and God. He encouraged praying together in small groups and even seemed to indicate that the power of prayer is magnified when we pray together. "Again, truly I tell you that if two of you on earth agree about anything you ask for, it will be done for you by my Father in heaven. For where two or three come together in my name, there am I with them" (Matthew 18:19-20). What a thought! Small groups are so important in God's economy that He promises to show up every time one meets.

In Acts 2, the early church's pattern of life consisted of two contexts. They met daily in the Temple courts. The details of those meetings are not clearly stated in the text, but the context would indicate those meetings were not unlike our Sunday services with a heavy emphasis on the apostles' teaching. In addition, they met regularly in homes for food, fellowship, and quite probably worship. From the beginning, the church met not only in larger group settings but also in small group settings (see Acts 2:42-47; 5:42).

The writer of Hebrews urged Christians to "consider how we may spur one another on toward love and good deeds. Let us not give up meeting together, as some are in the habit of doing, but let us encourage one another—and all the more as you see the Day approaching" (Hebrews 10:24-25). While this passage does not specifically indicate small groups, the purposes of meeting together as listed in the passage are best served in small group settings. The larger the group the more difficult it is to encourage one another. In small groups we can more effectively "spur one another on toward love and good deeds."

Small Groups Are Frequently at the Nexus of Great Movements

Throughout church history, vibrant small group life can be found in the places and eras of great spiritual achievement. One could argue that small groups spawned many of the great missionary movements and revivals in the Western world. It was at a small group meeting, a Christian Society meeting at Aldersgate, that John Wesley was transformed from a rigid religionist to a passionate follower of Jesus.

In the early 1800s a multifaceted world mission movement was birthed at the twice-weekly "Haystack Prayer Meetings" held in Sloan's Meadow in Connecticut. Each of the five regular participants made profound contributions to the cause of Christ. One of the students, Samuel J. Mills, helped found the American Bible Society and the United Foreign Missionary Society.

The "New Lights" small group meetings at Yale University and various Connecticut communities injected evangelistic zeal into American Calvinism and nurtured David Brainard's passion to evangelize the Native Americans of New England and western New York.

In 1928, when Henrietta Mears became Director of Christian Education at Hollywood Presbyterian Church, she took over a Sunday school of four hundred fifty and built it into one of six thousand five hundred. But it was the small group she founded, called "The Fellowship of the Burning Heart," that produced such leaders as Billy Graham, Bill Bright, Louis Evans Jr., Jim Rayburn, and Richard C. Halverson.[1] While only one example from a potential pool of thousands, "The Fellowship of the Burning Heart" is a dramatic example of a small group at the nexus of numerous great movements.

Small Groups in Healthy, Effective Churches Today

Real Life Ministries is a relatively new church in Post Falls, Idaho.[2] Real Life was built on a biblical and theological conviction that the Christian life is all about relationships. Nothing matters more than our relationships with Jesus Christ, other Christians, and unchurched, unbelieving people. Small groups are at the heart of Real Life's being. Over the years I have heard churches declare, "We are not a church with small groups, we are a church of small groups." Real Life can say that with honesty and integrity. They are an outstanding example of how a church grows by staying small.

Depending on the time of year, Real Life's attendance is between seven thousand two hundred and eight thousand per weekend. According to Aaron Couch, one of Real Life's founding pastors, during the summer of 2006 worship attendance was a bit over six thousand two hundred and small group participation was slightly over six thousand one hundred per week. How does this happen at Real Life? How could this happen in your church?

Every week, during every weekend service, Real Life mentions small groups not once but multiple times, and encourages people to participate. It may be an announcement, an illustration in the teaching, or a part of an individual's faith story shared with the congregation. It may be a parting reminder to folks who are not already a part of a small group to stop by the small groups table in the lobby and pick a group that suits them. In a variety of ways, Real Life prioritizes small groups.

Real Life prioritizes small groups in its staffing, both paid and volunteer. The church has a *Lobby Team* whose task is to identify new people, greet them, and guide them to the small group sign-up area. They train *Lobby Team* members to be effective in engaging new people and linking them to small group participation at Real Life. They have two staff people to enter small group participation information into their database so they can track everyone's small group participation. They have eleven paid staff in the area of small groups. They have four for worship and music.

Real Life is organized for small group success. The congregation is divided into seven *communities* that are geographically based. Each has an ordained or licensed pastor over it. The pastors recruit, train, supervise, and equip coaches. Each coach recruits, trains, supervises, and equips the leaders of two or three small groups. Each small group has a leader and typically consists of ten to twenty people. It is in these small groups that teaching, training, fellowship, care, and accountability happen. They study together, pray together, eat together, and often play together.

In addition to these *Home Groups*, Real Life has a wide variety of recovery groups. The church carries out its world mission involvement through small groups called *Huts*[3] that promote mission, organize short-term mission involvement, and act as communication links between the church and their missionaries. Small groups, called *Teams*, which are organized around missional purposes, lead most of their ministries.

Real Life Ministries owes it effectiveness and growth to small groups. They are a wonderful example of healthy, effective small group life in today's context. "Oh yeah," you might say, "it's easy for them to have that kind of a small group ministry. After all, look at how large they are." You could say that, but you would be missing the point. They don't have that kind of small group ministry because they are large. They became large because they stayed small, and emphasizing small groups was the strategy God blessed to help them grow until they became large.

Getting the Most Out of Your Small Groups

Pay Attention to Your Organizing Principles

If you want your small groups to have a profoundly positive impact on your church's health and effectiveness, you must pay attention to your organizing principles. Every group has an organizing principle, a purpose or a function for which the group was organized. People are attracted to or turned off by groups because of their organizing principles. There are people who are attracted to hiking groups, investment groups, or scrapbooking groups. Others are attracted to cooking classes, fantasy football groups, quilting groups, or spelunking groups. To use an old phrase, it's "different strokes for different folks."

What are the most common organizing principles for small groups in churches? By far, the two most common are fellowship and Bible study. Other common purposes include prayer, accountability, and music. Evangelism and ministry are the least common organizing principles. They should be the most common!

Churches inadvertently limit small group participation by failing to offer a variety of groups organized around different interests and purposes. They may have many small groups, but all are formed around Bible study or fellowship. Some churches have a smattering of prayer and accountability groups, but overall the vast majority are Bible study or fellowship groups.

Every church I know that is successful in incorporating a high percentage of its people into small groups offers an extensive menu of small groups organized around a wide and balanced array of purposes.

New Hope Christian Fellowship Oahu

New Hope Christian Fellowship Oahu in Honolulu, Hawaii, highlights eighty-eight small group opportunities on its Web site. The eighty-eight include a dance group, a group for adult children of divorce, a fibromyalgia support group, and a group for engaged couples anticipating marriage. *LifeChange* is a small group that helps believers come to a deeper understanding of salvation, live a balanced life based on God's Word, and understand their ongoing freedom in Christ. The church provides many options for new people to find a place that fits them in small group settings.

Some of the eighty-eight groups are umbrellas for numerous subgroups such as *Rebuilders*, a Christ-centered twelve-step and support group ministry. *Rebuilders* offers groups for individuals with alcohol and drug addictions; children of divorce; divorced adults; women experiencing domestic violence; adults dealing with anger issues, abortion, eating disorders, grief, or homosexuality; and parents of difficult or out-of-control children.

Here's what I mean by balance. Of the eighty-eight groups highlighted, forty-seven are ministry groups. They are organized for the primary purpose of doing ministry together. In their doing of ministry, they experience community, care, and accountability as natural by-products of their life together in ministry. Most of them engage in Bible study and exercise the discipline of prayer as part of their small group life. These vital small group functions happen not because the group was organized to provide them but as natural outcomes of grouping together to do ministry.

National Community Church

National Community Church in Washington, DC, meets in three locations.[4] It has become a magnet for many bright, young adults who work in various nooks and crannies of our government and government-related entities. The church's profound impact on the lives of these young adults and upon the residents of Washington comes partly through its worship and teaching ministry but primarily through its small groups.

This church declares its philosophy of small groups as, "Following Christ is a journey, and we have discovered that the journey is better when we walk alongside others and do life together. At NCC, we do life together and take the next steps in our spiritual journeys through small groups. Find a group and begin your journey today." When I visited the church's Web site, I found a twenty-page magazine of information about small groups organized around interests such as basketball, biking, tennis, running, ultimate Frisbee, dance, and theater as well as discipleship, Christian book studies, and spiritual disciplines such as Bible study and prayer. They have small groups that minister to the elderly, the homeless, people with HIV/AIDS, and the hungry. Other small groups address social justice issues and international poverty. These mission-ministry-outreach groups are focused on the community and world. In addition, there are internal ministry groups that minister through prayer, hospitality, worship, children's ministry, and so forth.

I have studied the growth dynamics of many churches over the years, including the role of small groups. Real Life Ministries, New Hope Christian Fellowship of Oahu, and National Community Church are just a few churches experiencing health, vitality, and effectiveness in large part because of small groups. Each emphasizes small groups. Each has groups organized around a wide range of purposes. Each church focused on small groups early in its history, while the church was still small. I believe that a fundamental element in the successful growth of these churches has been their commitment to small groups.

Be Wise Strategists

If you are a pastor or lay leader that needs to expand your small group ministry, and you seek to include more small groups with a wider assortment of organizing principles, you will need to proceed with great wisdom. Being a change agent is, in most churches, a dangerous occupation. Introducing small groups organized around evangelism and ministry in churches that currently have none will often be met with misunderstanding and opposition.

Forget about Altering DNA

Don't bother trying to introduce evangelistic or ministry purposes to existing groups. Sometimes in consulting with churches that have extensive small group ministry organized around Bible study, fellowship, prayer, and accountability, I listen as the leaders explain how they are now going to inject a *mission* or *ministry* component into their small groups. They say, "We are now expecting our groups to take on mission projects," or "We are now asking them to focus on ministry." What I have learned is that this approach nearly always causes tremendous amounts of stress among group members and ultimately ends in failure. The new thing, mission or ministry, is not what they "signed on for" when they first joined the group. It feels to them like a "bait and switch," and no one likes it when that happens.

When people join a group for a specific purpose, it is very difficult to impose another, quite different purpose on them. You can force compliance, but the moment you ease the pressure, the group will revert back to its original organizing principle. You will find it far more strategic and productive to start new groups that are, from the beginning, organized around mission and ministry purposes.

When Small Groups Go Bad

Sometimes small groups can be a negative influence in churches. Some small groups become self-centered, self-serving, and inward focused. They often become political power centers that keep the church from being outward focused and missional. When they are inward focused but benign, leaders should simply "refuse to feed them," letting them die a natural death over time. There's no need to vilify them or disband such groups, but neither do you promote them, give them preference, or invest budget money to preserve them. In addition, leaders should have the courage to refuse to heed them when their self-centeredness demands the church give them primary attention over the unbelieving and unchurched.

Some groups over time become cesspools of gossip, slander, and backbiting. They are no longer benign, and they begin infecting others with their negativity. The group and especially its leader(s) should be confronted, called to confession and repentance. If the group refuses, it should be disbanded.

Keep Your Counting Simple

Counting small group participation is not rocket science. It is not that hard to measure the percentage of your people who are involved in the small group life of your church. The only error a church can make in this area is to make it too complicated. I have watched church leaders go through all kinds of contortions trying to decide what groups count as small groups. Is the choir a small group? Is the choir a ministry group?

One way to define small groups is to ask the following: Does the group put people into relationship with a small enough number of people that they can be known, cared for, encouraged, challenged, taught, helped, and held accountable by the others in the group? If the group is small enough to do these things and is doing these things, call it a small group. If a person participates in the life of that group with a reasonable measure of regularity, count him or her as a small group participant. Keep it simple.[5]

The only complexity that might prove helpful to track is counting how many small groups exist in each of the major categories of organizing principles. How many are organized primarily for spiritual disciplines and growth? How many for evangelistic purposes? How many around interests? How many have recovery as their primary purpose? How many are organized to do mission and ministry? How many are focused inward (on the church and its people) and how many are focused outward (on the community, the world, the unchurched and unbelieving)? And what percentage of people are involved in each of these categories? Adding this layer of complexity, if you choose to do so, can help ensure that you are offering a broad range of small group opportunities and that you have people involved in both inward and outward focused small groups.

CHAPTER EIGHT

WHAT'S MORE IMPORTANT THAN DOLLARS?

Understandably, churches focus a lot on money. Unfortunately, the focus is so intense in enough churches that many unchurched people argue, "All the church cares about is my money."

Fred Craddock tells a powerful story demonstrating this from his own life. His mother had a deep commitment to Jesus and the church. She regularly took Fred and his siblings to church and Sunday school. His father did not share his wife's love for the church. He not only refused to attend, he often railed against the church, dismissing it as viewing him as nothing more than a statistic and a pledge. He did not believe the church really cared about him or anyone for that matter.

Fred Craddock's dad contracted cancer. His throat had been surgically removed. He was burned from the x-ray treatment. He couldn't eat and he couldn't speak. He weighed less than eighty pounds. Fred went to visit him in the hospital. The room was full of potted plants and cut flower arrangements. A high stack of cards sat beside his bed. Every flower, every card was from someone or some group from the church.

His dad watched him read through the cards. Since he couldn't speak he wrote on the side of a tissue box one line from Shakespeare. He wrote, "In this harsh world, draw your breath in pain to tell my story." Fred asked him, "What's your story, Daddy?" His father wrote, "I was wrong."[1]

Quite obviously, embracing the unbelieving skeptics at their point of need is more important than dollars. Being the hands, feet, and heart of Jesus is more important than money. Mission and ministry trump all else, or at least they should. Being the church, as Christ meant it to be, doing what He created the church to do is clearly more important than dollars. So first, ministry, being the presence and blessing of God, is more important than money.

Second, stewardship is more important than dollars. If money were the thing, Jesus would have honored the major donors and big givers, not the widow and her two small coins.

> As he looked up, Jesus saw the rich putting their gifts into the temple treasury. He also saw a poor widow put in two very small copper coins. "I tell you the truth," he said, "this poor widow has put in more than all the others. All these people gave their gifts out of their wealth; but she out of her poverty put in all she had to live on." (Luke 21:1-4)

Biblical stewardship encompasses more than the mere stewardship of money. The Bible teaches a total life stewardship. God has first claim on all we are, all we do, and all we have. We are to be good stewards of our calendars as well as our checkbooks. Our efforts and abilities are His to use for His purposes.

On that Judgment Day when Christians stand before God, we will give an account for our stewardship. How have we lived our lives? Have we invested our God-given time, God-given talents, and God-given treasure for His purposes? Did we feed Him, give Him water, and clothe Him? Did we tend to Him in His sickness; visit Him in prison? Have we been good stewards of every opportunity to minister to the needs of "the least of these" (Matthew 25:31-40)? In James 4:17, the failure to do good is called sin.

Just about everything else is more important than dollars; in God's economy people can give great sums of money and still be judged as lacking if they have not been faithful stewards of all in life (1 Corinthians 3:11-15; Revelation 20:11-15).

Still, in this chapter we are dealing with the stewardship of money. Some might protest that stewardship is about all of life. They are correct in that observation. In a previous chapter we dealt with measuring the non-monetary aspects of stewardship. Ministry involvement is a way of measuring our stewardship of time and talent. In this chapter, we focus on measuring our stewardship of the financial treasure entrusted to us by God.

You Mean There's More to It than Income?

If there is one thing all churches count, it is money! Or, more accurately, all churches count income. Even churches that have stopped counting everything else will still count the dollars that come in. I have assessed churches that cannot tell me how many people have attended worship for years, haven't counted baptisms in a decade, and have no idea how much money has been spent on what. But they can tell me exactly to the penny how much came in. Invariably, in these churches, the amount coming in is less than the budget calls for, and so there is a history of cutting programs, ministries, and missionary support.

Counting income makes sense. If the money does not come in, you cannot spend it. Budgets aside, the only way to know how much money you can spend is to know how much money came in. Counting income is necessary, but when it comes to measuring a church's effectiveness in financial stewardship, there is something far more significant to count. The most important and strategic thing to measure is tithing.

Tithing?

Some of you are saying, "Tithing? The most important thing to measure is tithing? I don't even believe in tithing." Many pastors and lay leaders refuse to preach and teach tithing because they believe tithing is an Old Testament concept, a requirement under the Old Testament Law. Their logic, "Since we live in New Testament times, under a new covenant with God and no longer under the Law, we should not teach people to tithe. Tithing does not apply to us today." I believe they have the facts right, but make the wrong conclusion from the facts.

Under the Law

Tithing, or the giving of one-tenth of all we *possess*, is an Old Testament concept. It was the Law. God required His people in that day and age to tithe.

> A tithe of everything from the land, whether grain from the soil or fruit from the trees, belongs to the LORD; it is holy to the LORD. Whoever would redeem any of their tithe must add a fifth of the value to it. Every tithe of the herd and flock—every tenth animal that passes under the shepherd's rod—will be holy to the LORD. (Leviticus 27:30-32 TNIV)

85

In Nehemiah's day, Jerusalem was in shambles. The city and its walls had been destroyed. Its population had been decimated. Nehemiah's success in rebuilding the city relied heavily on the people's tithing. Everyone, even the priests (the Levites), gave one-tenth of their possessions (Nehemiah 10:28-39). Tithing was so much a part of their religious fabric that Nehemiah asked the people to tithe not only their possessions but also themselves. And the people responded.

> Now the leaders of the people settled in Jerusalem. The rest of the people cast lots to bring one out of every ten of them to live in Jerusalem, the holy city, while the remaining nine were to stay in their own towns. The people commended all who volunteered to live in Jerusalem. (Nehemiah 11:1-2 TNIV)

Under the Law, tithing was both expected and practiced.

Under Grace

As Christians, we are no longer bound by all the laws in the Old Testament such as dietary prohibitions, the celebration of Passover, and Yom Kippur. According to Paul, the Law provides knowledge of sin, but it is not through the Law that Christians find salvation (Romans 3:19-20). Through Christ's death on the cross we no longer must rely on the works of the Law for salvation (Galatians 3:10-13). Paul's message is that we have been freed from the penalty and control of sin by God's grace.

> In the same way, count yourselves dead to sin but alive to God in Christ Jesus. Therefore do not let sin reign in your mortal body so that you obey its evil desires. Do not offer the parts of your body to sin, as instruments of wickedness, but rather offer yourselves to God, as those who have been brought from death to life; and offer the parts of your body to him as instruments of righteousness. For sin shall not be your master, because you are not under law, but under grace. (Romans 6:11-14; see also Ephesians 2:8-10)

As Christians, we believe that God's forgiving and saving grace through Jesus Christ gives rise to a life lived out of gratitude to God for His generosity and blessing. By His mercy, God does not give us the punishment we deserve for our sinful choices. By His grace, God gives us blessings we do not deserve. And so we give to God that which represents our gratitude for His grace. In fact, the measure of our gratefulness often reflects our understanding of His generosity. We learn to be generous with God because of His generosity with us.

How does this relate to tithing? The connection is in this question: Why would we ever consider giving God *less*, living in the light of His grace and generosity, than we were required to give Him under the Law? If we were expected to give a tenth before His gracious generosity was so lavishly demonstrated in Jesus, why would we want to give Him less now that we know He gave His very life for us?

The Bible speaks not only of tithes but also of offerings, sacrifices, and special gifts. Deuteronomy 12:11 reads, "Then to the place the LORD your God will choose as a dwelling for his Name—there you are to bring everything I command you: your burnt offerings and sacrifices, your tithes and special gifts, and all the choice possessions you have vowed to the LORD."

Pause and think of the gifts of God's grace—health, strength, food, all of nature to enjoy, loved ones, and above all eternal salvation. Such generosity on His part should lead us to begin with a tithe, not stop with it or, worse yet, contemplate giving less than a tenth.

Though no longer demanded of us, the tithe still has meaning. Those of us who understand God's grace and generosity in our lives should consider the tithe as the foundation of our giving. Tithing and more should be the norm for mature Christians. Tithing is one indicator of spiritual maturity. If your church is in the business of making mature disciples, you will be intentional about raising up Christ-followers who tithe.

Remember It's All His

Helping people learn to tithe joyfully (2 Corinthians 9:7) begins with reminding them that everything belongs to God. The Bible makes this point abundantly clear. Psalm 24:1 declares, "The earth is the LORD's and all that is in it." Elsewhere the psalmist reminds us that God owns "the cattle on a thousand hills" regardless of who is tending them (Psalm 50:10-11). "'The silver is mine and the gold is mine,' declares the LORD Almighty" (Haggai 2:8). The apostle Paul declared, "All things were created by him and for him" (Colossians 1:16). Paul later asks a piercing question, "What do you have that you did not receive?" (1 Corinthians 4:7). The writer of Deuteronomy cautioned, "You may say to yourself, 'My power and the strength of my hands have produced this wealth for me.'

But remember the LORD your God, for it is he who gives you the ability to produce wealth" (Deuteronomy 8:17-18).

Perspective and attitudes begin to change as we realize that it all belongs to God. He owns it all. He has given us from what is His, a portion to manage as His stewards. One hundred percent of all He has given us is His, not ours; our managerial or custodial task is to discern how He wants it spent.[2]

If we believe in the first place that everything belongs to God, then returning to Him one-tenth or more is not all that hard. Rather than grousing because we *must* give God one-tenth, we can rejoice in that He only expects a portion of it back. Here is still another indication of His generosity. He allows us to keep the majority of what is rightfully His.

Teaching People to Tithe and More

During my years as pastor in the parish setting, I took the responsibility of helping people become tithers. What follows are the recurring themes I taught. These are the principles of stewardship I urge churches to consider when I'm asked to consult with them in financial areas.

Stewardship Principles

Start with a tithe. The base for your giving is one-tenth of what you make. You plant your feet firmly on the floor of financial stewardship when you give a tithe. One-tenth is the floor, not the ceiling.

Work toward a tithe. If you have not previously been tithing, you may have made choices that make an immediate adjustment to a tithe improper or impossible. If that is your situation, then start with the highest percentage you can manage. Over time, incrementally increase your giving until you reach a tithe.

Get out of debt. If you cannot afford to tithe because you are servicing debt, get out of debt as quickly as possible. Once out of debt, stay out of debt. Accept debt only when necessary to purchase appreciating assets, most frequently your home.

Tithe to your church. Your tithe belongs to your church. I often express it this way: "Where you eat is where you pay. If you eat at Wendy's, you do not pay at McDonald's; you pay at Wendy's." If your church is feeding you and your loved ones, caring for you, and giving you opportunity to grow in your faith and to serve God, then that is where your tithe should go.

Give more than a tithe. Give offerings above the tithe as God prompts and enables you. Offerings may go to special projects and ministries at your church, or they may be given to other organizations, missionaries, or ministries as God leads you to give.

Be a cheerful giver. Don't give so God will "owe you" and give to you. Don't give to relieve guilt or to make yourself look good in others' eyes. Let your giving reflect the gratitude in your heart to God for His grace and generosity poured out in your life. Delight in giving is found when we give out of gratitude.

The pastor and staff must model "a tithe and more" giving. Teaching is more than talking. We teach best when we do what we tell others to do. A pastor or member of the church's staff does not have the right to teach tithing if he or she is not tithing. If you are going to teach "a tithe and more" giving then practice "a tithe and more" giving.

Lay leaders must model "a tithe and more" giving. If a leader does not lead, he or she is not a leader. Leadership means doing what you want others to do. A person who is not willing to be obedient to God in stewardship of money does not have the right to decide for others in a leadership role. A person who does not demonstrate a commitment to the mission and vision of the church by giving a tithe and more does not have the right to occupy leadership positions in that church.

Lift the veil of secrecy. Many people and churches shroud giving records in a manner that makes the Cold War's Iron Curtain look porous. In seeking to keep Jesus' admonition against publicly strutting our giving (Matthew 6:2-4), they mandate that no one should know. Some seminaries teach pastors that they should not know who gives or how much those people give since it might tempt them to be partial toward big givers. First, it is impossible for no one to know who gives and at least in general terms how much they give. Counters, financial secretaries, data entry people, and others know at least bits and pieces. Second, everyone (including the pastor) makes assumptions about how much people give, and attitudes are influenced by their suppositions. Better for pastors to know and adjust their behavior to reality than to try to adjust to what may or may not be reality.

I am not arguing for a completely open book when it comes to giving records, although I do have experience with that. My first pastorate was in a rural church where each family was *apportioned* an amount that the family was expected to give toward the support of the church and its ministries. Mission offerings and special projects were additional, but the apportionments assured that the basic operational costs of the church would be covered. Apportionments were based on the church's anticipated needs, and each family was assessed based on its ability to pay. Established farming families were expected to pay more than young families just getting started in farming. Most interesting of all was the annual report in which each family's apportioned amount and their actual giving were noted for all to see. Making budget was never a problem in that church! I *do not* recommend this approach.

What I *do* advocate is that the pastor should know who gives and how much they give. Furthermore, I believe that the church should know what the pastor's family gives to the church. I regularly urge pastors to annually announce their giving for the past year and their intention to give for the coming year. Such an approach models good stewardship and brings accountability in giving to the church's leadership community. No one gets to hide poor stewardship behind a veil of secrecy.

Following Jesus' Example

You need not apologize for talking about money and teaching people how to manage what God has entrusted to them. Jesus frequently taught about giving and never with an apology. He was direct, matter-of-fact, and clear.

Jesus taught that an attachment to money can keep us from eternal life (Matthew 19:16-26). He warned that we can give money legalistically but that if we do not have a passion for justice, mercy, and forgiveness, we risk His judgment (Matthew 23:23-24). He warned us, "No one can serve two masters. Either you will hate the one and love the other, or you will be devoted to the one and despise the other. You cannot serve both God and Money" (Matthew 6:24 TNIV). He cautioned against becoming fretful about money (Matthew 6:25-33).

Some of Jesus' teaching constituted a course in Money Management 101. "Suppose one of you wants to build a tower. Won't you first sit down and estimate the cost to see if you have enough money to complete it? For if you lay the foundation and are not able to finish it, everyone who sees it will ridicule you, saying, 'This person began to build and wasn't able to finish'" (Luke 14:28-30 TNIV). The parable of the talents clearly communicates the money management principle that God blesses those who take the money He gives them and invest it in ways that produce a Kingdom return (Matthew 25:14-28).

Jesus found it important to talk directly and often with His followers about money. If we want to be effective in helping people grow as disciples of Jesus, we must teach them about money just as He did.[3]

There's More than One Way to Measure

If you are serious about effectively raising up mature financial stewards, you will establish an ongoing system of stewardship education that includes all aspects of stewardship. There are two ways by which you can measure your church's effectiveness in this area. You can measure what percentage of people tithe, or you can measure to what extent your church as a whole tithes.

A Church of Tithers

The method for measuring the percentage of people who tithe is simple. You ask them. You create a discreet process by which all are asked to indicate whether or not they tithe. It's as simple as asking, "Do you tithe?" They answer yes or no, and you take them at their word. The ideal would be 100 percent of households answering yes truthfully.[4] I know of no church that even approaches the ideal of 100 percent. So how do you set an appropriate goal?

The process begins with establishing your current percentage of tithers. How many households make up your church constituency? How many of them reported that they tithe based on their household income? Divide the number reporting that they tithe by the total number of households in your church, and you will have your current status. This becomes the benchmark against which your future effectiveness in growing tithers is measured.[5]

In your first year, establish a SMART[6] goal that projects a higher percentage of tithing households than your benchmark. Over time, 50 percent or more tithing households would be an achievement worth celebrating. I urge you to strive for 66 percent or more. If two-thirds or more of your church families give a tithe or more, you can sponsor workshops and seminars, and people will beat a path to your doorstep.

A Tithing Church

Measuring the degree to which you are a tithing church is also relatively simple. Research and discover the average annual household income for the communities included in your parish area. Multiply the average household income by the number of actual households in your congregation. If your church is representative of your community, this figure will be the composite income for the church. Divide the actual contribution income for the year by the church's composite income and you will calculate the percent actually given to the church. Compare that figure to 10 percent to learn to what extent you are actually a tithing church.

To illustrate, let's assume the average household income in your parish area is $64,525. If your church has 120 households, the church's composite income will be about $7,743,000. Again for the sake of illustration, let's assume your church's actual contribution income was $305,500. Divide $305,500 by $7,743,000 and the church as a whole is giving about 3.9 percent.

In recent years I have heard figures ranging from 1.6 percent to 2.4 percent cited as the average household's annual giving to the church here in the United States. I have not seen any figure I consider definitive. In my consulting, I tell churches that they should initially aim to raise that figure to 4 percent,[7] then 5 percent, then 6 percent. If they ever exceed 6 percent, they can write the books, hold the seminars, and the people will come!

CHAPTER NINE

WHAT PRODUCT ARE YOU PRODUCING ANYWAY?

W ise and effective leaders start with the end in sight. Did you ever try to get somewhere when you did not know where *somewhere* was? Whether you are using handwritten directions, a Google map, or a GPS system, you must know the address in order to get there.

Your *mission, vision, objectives,* and *goals* are like addresses, each more specific and focused than the last. Your *mission* is the purpose for which God created you. Your *vision* is a word picture of what it will look like when you arrive at your missional destination. An *objective* is something you intend to attain. To declare it as an objective implies you believe it is attainable, and you will do the things required to achieve it. *Goals* are the specific, measurable milestones established to guide you on your way to accomplishing your objective.

Many churches work hard to articulate their mission and vision. They proudly display their mission and vision statements, but little or nothing changes. Some can even recite the statements but still do not achieve anything even faintly resembling them. In time, the statements are ignored and forgotten. Eventually, the church sours on the very idea of having a vision. "We tried that once, and it didn't work." So what is the problem? Is having a vision unnecessary? Is writing mission and/or vision statements irrelevant and pointless? I don't believe so.

A clear understanding of your mission is the foundation of effective ministry. A well-conceived vision and a well-written vision statement are fundamental to understanding where you are going as a church. They are essential to seeing the end you need to keep in sight if you have any hope of arriving there.

To use a travel metaphor, your vision identifies the city where you are headed. Recently, I wanted to get to a meeting in Pasadena. I entered "Pasadena" into my GPS. The wise, all-knowing program resident in my GPS unit asked me an important question. Did I want Pasadena, California, or Pasadena, Texas? Knowing not only the city, but also the state is critical to my arriving at the location I have in mind. Your mission identifies the right state.

Important as it is to know the city and state, if that's all I know it is unlikely I will ever reach my destination. The problem with churches that find well-written mission and vision statements ineffective and irrelevant is that they still do not know where they are going. They do not know the address.

An objective is like a street address. If my GPS is going to direct me to my destination, I must program in the street address. If I do not know the street address, I must give it a business name or landmark so it can identify a street address. Bottom line, without a street address, you will never arrive. In my experience, very few churches ever clearly articulate even their primary objective. When have we arrived at our vision? When have we completed our mission? When is our job done? You will never satisfactorily answer those questions until you have articulated your objective.

Goals and action steps are like the succession of highways and roads you take to arrive at your destination or your objective. Keeping the end in sight requires a thorough understanding of your vision and your primary objective. Then you can establish the goals and articulate the action steps needed in order to reach your objective and fulfill your vision. At this point, the only thing required for ministry effectiveness is actually working your plan. Your plan is accomplished by completing your action steps.

So what is your church's primary, overarching objective? Answering that question begs another question.

What *Business* Are You In?

Many pastors and even some lay leaders bristle anytime church and business are linked. They find all this talk about mission and vision state-

ments, objectives, and goals deeply disturbing. "A church is not a business," they say emphatically. "It's a ministry, a spiritual entity created by
God to do His work on earth." This is true. A church is not a business,
but that does not mean there aren't important similarities.

The primary objections to comparing a church with a business are theological and spiritual. God created the church and commissioned it to
make disciples (Matthew 28:18-20). God declares His ownership of the
church and pledges to make it strong and effective (Matthew 16:18). Paul
said Jesus is the head of the church (Colossians 1:18) and called the
church Christ's body (1 Corinthians 12:12-17; Colossians 1:24). From
this perspective, the church worldwide, as well as its local expressions, is
nothing at all like a business. It would be a travesty to reduce something
so grand and majestic to the same stature as a mere business.

There is a second, very practical motivation for many pastors reacting
against the comparing of churches and business. Countless pastors have
suffered significant battering and bruising from laypeople who want the
church to run like a business. What they usually want is for ministry out-
lays and missionary support to be cut in order to keep spending in line
with income. Or they want the pastor to operate under the board's direction with the pastor merely implementing the board's wishes. Being
budget-driven rather than mission- and vision-driven always stunts the
effectiveness and growth of a church. Being board led rather than pastor
led will similarly stunt the ministry effectiveness of most churches. I am
not, therefore, encouraging churches to be businesslike in this sense of
the word. But ministry effectiveness does require asking and answering a
few vital businesslike questions.

Peter Drucker was probably the most respected business analyst and
business philosopher of the twentieth century. He was also a devout
Christian and committed churchman. Especially in his later years, he
offered his business wisdom to leaders of non-profits of all kinds, but especially churches. Drucker was famous for asking business and church leaders alike the question, "What business are you in?" His profoundly simple
premise was, if you do not know what business you are in, you cannot succeed at it. If you do not have a clue what you are supposed to do, you will
not excel at what you do.[1]

Many churches achieve little in the way of ministry because they cannot
articulate the essence of their ministry. What is the purpose for which your
church exists? What is your church's mission? If the pastor, lay leaders, and
ministry leaders cannot clearly articulate their church's mission, then the

church is doomed to mediocrity at best. When God established the church, what was the church's business? What *product* is the church to make?

A Common Mission

Churches do not get the privilege of choosing their purpose from a long list of options. Churches do not get the privilege of deciding what business they are in. God decided the church's business. God clearly identified the product the church is to produce, namely mature followers of Jesus Christ.

> Therefore go and make disciples of all nations, baptizing them in the name of the Father and of the Son and of the Holy Spirit, and teaching them to obey everything I have commanded you. (Matthew 28:19-20)

In your going...as you go...whenever you go...wherever you go...as often as you go...however you go...for whatever reasons you go...no matter with whom you go...make disciples. The church of Jesus Christ is in the disciple-making business.

That the church's purpose is already spelled out is no secret. It's no mystery. Every church shares a common purpose with every other church. Its purpose, or mission, is to make disciples. While each church must state its purpose in language that is meaningful to its people, the mission statement must be about making disciples because that is the church's God-given business.

Arguably, today's best-known church mission statement is Willow Creek's "to turn irreligious people into fully devoted followers of Jesus." This is an excellent mission statement, mostly because it is about making disciples. Beyond that, it is brief and is stated in everyday language; therefore it is memorable. If you can remember and recite your church's mission statement, you are more likely to actually live by it.

Many churches have simply *borrowed* Willow Creek's mission statement. While I believe churches benefit from the process of stating their mission in their own way, it is better to borrow a good mission statement than to write a poor one.

A Specific Vision

Vision statements, however, are a different story. The manner in which Willow Creek (with its history, size, location, leaders, and theological nuances) accomplishes its mission will look quite different from the manner in which other churches, even the ones that use Willow Creek's mission statement, accomplish their mission. Each church's vision is a focusing and narrowing of its understanding of its mission that enables it to accomplish that mission more effectively.

Remember, a ministry vision is a word picture of what it looks like as you accomplish your mission. What it looks like when one church becomes effective at making disciples might not look the same at another church. Therefore vision statements tend to be more diverse, more unique, and more church-specific.

In a Nutshell

As individual Christians and as churches we are in the disciple-making business. If our God-given mission is to make disciples, our *products* must be mature followers of Jesus Christ. Any church that is doing what God created it to do will be found helping people become mature Christ-followers. All this leads to another crucial question. How do you know if you are producing mature disciples? Are you succeeding at making mature Christ-followers?

What Does a Mature Disciple Look Like?

In the travel or trip analogy, your mission declares the state where you want to arrive. Your vision identifies the town or city. Your objective, to produce mature disciples, is the street address. Your overarching objective as a church is your destination. You have arrived as a church when you are effective at helping people become mature followers of Jesus.

We are now at another juncture where pastors and lay leaders often balk at measuring. They declare, "You cannot measure spirituality!" Spirituality is internal and attitudinal. It's true; there are aspects of spiritual maturity no one but God can measure (Acts 15:8; Matthew 23:25-28; Luke 16:15). But the Bible frequently describes behaviors that indicate spiritual maturity. While there are literally hundreds of passages that bear out this point, let's look at one in particular.

In Galatians 5, the apostle Paul listed the fruit of the Spirit—the evidence that the Spirit of God is at work in a person's life and is having success in producing spiritual maturity. "But the fruit of the Spirit is love, joy, peace, patience, kindness, goodness, faithfulness, gentleness and self-control. Against such things there is no law" (Galatians 5:22-23). Each is readily observed in behavioral terms. For decades I have kept on my dresser a small piece of marble, imprinted with the words, "Love is a verb." Love is demonstrated behaviorally. The presence of joy is evidenced by what we say and do, even in the tough times. People who are at peace with God, themselves, and those around them look and act differently from those who are anxious. They are a calming presence in the midst of a maelstrom. Patience, kindness, goodness, faithfulness, gentleness, and self-control are all evident through behavior.

The reality is this. You can and must identify some specific characteristics or behaviors that indicate spiritual maturity. It is not necessary to capture all the biblical indicators or to have a perfect list of characteristics or behaviors. But it is necessary to have a list that reflects your church's theology, values, and ethos. And it is imperative that the list be measurable.

Describe the Disciples You Are Making in Measurable Terms

Perhaps an example of one church's work in this regard will help make this clear. Immanuel Church in Gurnee, Illinois, identifies four primary behavioral arenas, the first of which is drawing others to Christ.[2] For this church, a mature disciple is actively engaged in evangelism and outreach. It measures effectiveness as a church by the percentage of people who maintain a list of unchurched and unbelieving friends with whom they intentionally relate in order to bring them to church and to Christ. While there are many behaviors that would indicate a passion for reaching people for Christ, this church has chosen one highly specific behavior that correlates to a program of the church. This behavior is measurable.

Their second behavioral arena is participating in community with other Christ-followers. Measurable behaviors identified and tracked are regular worship attendance and regular participation in at least one small group of the church.

The third kind of behavior Immanuel Church wants to see in the lives of its people is serving others. If a person is involved in serving others in the church, community, or world, then this church considers itself to be effective in producing a mature disciple. In this way the church is achieving its objective.

Knowing and obeying Scripture is Immanuel Church's final behavioral arena, for which there are two measures. Are people involved in a disciplined, ongoing study of the Bible? And can they point to recent life changes that are attributable to their Bible study? If people are not only studying the Bible but also making it more than an intellectual exercise by incorporating new insight and understanding into their lives, Immanuel's leaders believe they are producing the kind of *product* their line of *business* calls for. They are reaching their overarching objective. They have arrived at their destination.

The Spiritually Mature Disciple

You must love the Lord your God with all your heart, all your soul, and all your mind. This is the first and greatest commandment. A second is equally important: Love your neighbor as yourself. (from Matthew 22:37-39)

The spiritually mature disciple at Immanuel demonstrates an increasing love for God and people by:

- Drawing others to Christ
    - maintains a list of unchurched/unbelieving friends with whom he or she intentionally relates in order to bring them to church and to Christ
- Participating in community with other Christ-followers
    - is regular in church attendance
    - participates regularly in a small group
- Living to serve others
    - serves people in the church
    - serves people in the community
    - serves people in another culture or country
- Knowing and obeying Scripture
    - is involved in disciplined, ongoing study of the Bible
    - can cite a recent change in thoughts, attitudes, or behavior as a result of his or her Bible study

---

As you read this list, you might be thinking, "They missed this one. They should have included this one instead of that one." This is normal. It's not that they are wrong or that you are right. It simply means that your church's list would be different. It should be different. It should be reflective of the uniqueness God has built into your congregation as opposed to the way He has molded Immanuel or any other church.

A Final Blessing

As I bring this book to a close, I would like the privilege of asking God's blessing on you and your church. It comes from my heart since I have no greater passion than to see churches effectively do what God intends for them to do. I want God's blessing on you and your church to be evident.

God bless you as you:

- Demonstrate your passion for the unbelieving and unchurched by regularly welcoming new believers into the family of God and your church through baptism and/or confirmation.
- Expand your influence by attracting more worshipers who attend with a high degree of regularity.
- Become increasingly effective at incorporating the visitors God brings you.
- Teach all to serve somewhere—in the church, community, or world.
- Raise up new leaders.
- Use small groups to bring transformational change and life-long growth in every constituent.
- Introduce each participant to the joy of generous giving.

In other words, God bless you as you fulfill your mission by making mature followers of Jesus.

APPENDIX: METRICS MANUAL— YOUR PRACTICAL GUIDE TO COUNTING WHAT COUNTS

These pages contain an overview of the metrics and measures covered in the book as well as instructions for each of the Excel™ worksheets that you can download at www.abingdonpress.com/downloads.

NOTE: The worksheet instructions shown below are also included in Comments boxes on each worksheet page of the Excel™ document on the CD. These Comments boxes can be moved, closed, or deleted as necessary:

1) To move a Comments box: Click on the edge of the box and drag it.
2) To close all Comments boxes in the spreadsheet: Go to View in the Menu Bar and click on Comments. All of the Comments boxes in the spreadsheet will close, and you will see a small red triangle in the corner of the cell where the Comments box is housed. To view Comments boxes: Go to View in the Menu Bar and click on Comments. All of the Comments boxes in the spreadsheet will now be visible.
3) To hide or view a single Comments box: Right click in the cell that houses the Comments box and choose Hide Comment or Show Comment.
4) To permanently delete a Comments box: Right click in the cell that houses the box (with the small red triangle in the corner) and choose Delete Comment.

Chapter 2: If You Could Count Only One Thing

Measuring Conversions

Instructions for Using the Conversions Worksheet:

1) To find the cost of conversions: Make two calculations, both of which start with the number of baptisms and/or confirmations. The numbers in columns B, C, D, and E are included for demonstration only.

2) The formula in column F calculates the cost in people: The average worship attendance for the year divided by the number of baptisms + confirmations. See the Worship Attendance tab for instructions on calculating average worship attendance.

3) The formula in column G calculates the cost in dollars: The total church income for the year divided by the number of baptisms + confirmations.

4) Customize the worksheet for the way your denomination or church considers conversion (e.g., add columns and calculations for adult vs. junior confirmations, membership by profession of faith, infant vs. adult baptism).

5) To add a new year to the table: Copy the row of the last year and paste into the next open row. Update the year label and erase the numbers in the first four columns.

Chapter 3: How Many and How Often?

Measuring Worship Attendance

Base Worship Attendance is calculated by dividing the total number of people counted in worship divided by the number of weeks in the designated time frame. A designated time frame may be a month, quarter, or year. See chapter 3.

Instructions for Using the Worship Attendance Worksheet:

1) YTD Total and Weekly Average columns contain formulas that will calculate when the Worship Attendance figure is added each week. The figure in cell D55 represents the Average Weekly Attendance for the sample year.

2) To add a new year: Copy columns A through D to a blank column to the right of the existing years in the worksheet. Delete the figures in the Worship Attendance column for the new year and replace the title "SAMPLE" with the year you are adding.

Market Share

Market Share is the church's Base Worship Attendance divided by the number of people living in your geographic parish area.

Instructions for Using the Market Share Worksheet:

1) The numbers entered in columns B and C are for demonstration purposes only.

2) Enter the Total Parish Area Population. Identify the communities where your members and attendees live. Identify any additional adjacent communities you could reach if you were intentional about it. Check current census data for each community; add them together to arrive at your church's parish area population. Recheck these figures each year to check for population shifts and trends.

3) Enter your current weekly average worship attendance. See the Worship Attendance tab for instructions on calculating this figure.

4) The formula in the "Percentage" box will automatically calculate your market share.

5) To add a year: Copy the entire row of the last year in the table and paste it into the next open row. Once you add the Year label and data, you can sort the table by column headings so that the years appear in order. You may want to go back and calculate your market share for previous years to help in establishing your benchmark.

Worship Frequency as a Measure of Commitment and/or Maturity

Monthly Average Attendance is calculated by dividing the number of unique worship attendees in a month by the total number of people counted in worship for that same month. "Unique Worship Attendee" means a person who attended worship at least once during the month. Each person is counted only once in the month regardless of how many weeks he or she attended.

Instructions for Using the Worship Frequency Worksheet:

1) Create one row per member and attendee. To add a row: Insert a blank row above the "New Name" row. Copy and paste the entire "New Name" row into the blank row. This will update the formulas and ensure that they continue to work properly.

2) Enter the last and first name of the new member or attendee. To see the worksheet in alphabetical order, select all but the Totals row and sort by last name.

3) Each week the person attends, enter a 1 in the column corresponding to that week. Formulas in the "Quarter" columns calculate the percentage of weeks that person attended year-to-date.

4) Totals row (shaded green): The number at the bottom of column B is the total number of members/attendees in your church. The totals at the bottom of each Week and Quarter column indicate the number of attendees for that Week and Year-to-date, respectively.

Chapter 4: How Many Stay?

Measuring Visitor Retention

Define "visitor." Typically a *visitor* for the purposes of measuring effectiveness at retention is "an unchurched or unbelieving person who attends our church and could attend our church on a regular basis if he or she chose to." In addition a visitor might be a churched and/or believing person who is new to the community or who for personal reasons chooses to begin attending our church on a periodic or regular basis.

Define assimilated using this criteria:
- Attends worship at least 60 percent of the time.
- Participates in at least one small group.
- Involved in at least one form of mission or ministry.
- The number of visitors meeting all three criteria divided by the total number of visitors equals the percentage of *fully assimilated* visitors.
- The number of visitors meeting only two of the criteria divided by the total number of visitors equals the percentage of *partially assimilated* visitors.
- The number of visitors meeting only one of the criteria divided by the total number of visitors equals the percentage of *initially assimilated* visitors.
- Aim at a *minimum* threshold of 30 percent fully assimilated visitors.

Instructions for Using the Visitor Retention Worksheet:

1) Define "visitor." Enter the name of each person meeting your criteria for a visitor. Enter the date of the person's initial visit to the church (or the date you first received his or her name and contact information).

2) **Attendance**: Determine how many times per month, on average, a person must attend worship to be considered assimilated (e.g., a minimum average of two weekends per month). When a person meets the attendance assimilation criteria, enter a 1 in the Attendance column for that person.

3) **Small Group**: When the person becomes involved in the life of a small group, enter a 1 in the Small Group column.

4) **Ministry**: When the person becomes involved in some aspect of ministry, enter a 1 in the Ministry column.

5) **Retained Visitor**: Determine the criteria for assimilation or retention (e.g., has met the criteria for 2 or 3 involvement categories: Attendance, Small Group, Ministry). When a visitor meets your criteria for assimilation or retention, enter a 1 in the Retained Visitor column.

6) **Retention Rate**: Choose an Initial Date range (e.g., 3 months or 1 year from first date to last). To find your church's retention rate for the chosen period: Add the numbers in the Retained Visitor column for the corresponding date range and divide the sum by the total number of visitors for the same period. For example, if you had 12 visitors within a three-month period, and 3 of those visitors met your criteria for assimilation, your church's retention rate would be 25 percent (3/12 = .25).

Chapter 5: How Many Serve?

Measuring Ministry Involvement

- Create a database of all attendees and members.
- Define "involved in ministry in the church."
    - Use either the one-tiered or two-tiered approach as introduced in chapter 5.
- Apply your definition of "involved" to each constituent in your database
- Use the Ministry Involvement–Church worksheet to calculate the percentage of people involved in ministry in the church.
- Establish a goal for increasing the percentage of people involved in the church.
    - Identify, recruit, and train people to serve God in the church
    - Empower them to find a place of service matching their gifts, passion, and sense of God's call on their lives.
- Define "involved in ministry in the community."
    - Survey your people to discover who is already involved in ministry in the community.
    - Train them to fully use their community involvement for spiritual as well as humanitarian purposes.
- Apply your definition of "involved" to each constituent in your database.
- Use the Ministry Involvement–Community worksheet to calculate the percentage of people involved in ministry in the community.
- Raise the value of serving God in the community in your church.
- Establish a goal for increasing the percentage of people involved in the church.
    - Identify, recruit and train people to serve God in the community.
    - Empower them to find a place of service matching their gifts, passion, and sense of God's call on their lives.
- Define "involved in ministry in the world."
- Use the Ministry Involvement–World worksheet to calculate the percentage of people involved in ministry in the world.
- Raise the value of serving God throughout the world.
- Establish a goal for increasing the percentage of people involved throughout the world. This goal is typically over five years or more.

○ Identify, recruit, and train people to serve God throughout the world.

○ Empower them to find a place of service matching their gifts, passion, and sense of God's call on their lives.

Instructions for Using the Ministry Involvement–Church Worksheet:

1) Define "involved." Determine the criteria for what constitutes involvement in your church's ministry. Adapt the table to your setting—revise column headings and add new columns. If you are not using a two-tiered system, delete columns K and L.

2) Enter the names of all members and attendees.

3) Enter a 1 in each column that applies for each person's ministry involvement.

4) If the person meets your definition of involved, enter a 1 in the Status column beside the name.

5) To find the percentage of people involved in ministry: Divide the sum of the numbers in the Status column by the total number of people listed. The formula in cell M1 has done this calculation for the sample shown. It will update as you enter your data.

Instructions for Using the Ministry Involvement–Community Worksheet:

1) Define "community ministry involvement." Determine the criteria for what constitutes involvement in your church's ministry in the community. Adapt the table to your setting—revise column headings and add new columns.

2) Copy and paste the names of all members and attendees from the Ministry Involvement–Church worksheet.

3) Enter a 1 in each column that applies for each person's ministry involvement.

4) If the person meets your definition of involved, enter a 1 in the Status column beside the name.

5) To find the percentage of people involved in community ministry: Divide the sum of the numbers in the Status column by the total number of people listed. The formula in cell L1 performs this calculation for the sample and will update as you enter data.

Instructions for Using the Ministry Involvement–World Worksheet:
1) Define "world ministry involvement." Determine the criteria for what constitutes involvement in your church's ministry in the world. Adapt the table to your setting—revise column headings and add new columns.
2) Copy and paste the names of all members and attendees from the Ministry Involvement–Church worksheet.
3) Enter a 1 in each column that applies for each person's ministry involvement.
4) If the person meets your definition of involved, enter a 1 in the Status column beside their name.
5) To find the percentage of people involved in world ministry: Divide the sum of the numbers in the Status column by the total number of people listed. The formula in cell I1 performs this calculation for the sample and will update as you enter data.

Instructions for Using the Ministry Involvement–Composite Worksheet:
1) Enter the total number of members and attendees in cell A2. In the sample, the formula in A2 counts the number of last names entered in the Ministry Involvement–Church worksheet.
2) **Serving in Church:** Enter the total number of members and attendees who meet your established criteria for Ministry Involvement in the Church. In the sample, the formula in cell B2 adds the numbers in the Status column of the Ministry Involvement–Church worksheet.
3) **Serving in the Community:** Enter the total number of members and attendees who meet your established criteria for Ministry Involvement in the Community. In the sample, the formula in D2 adds the numbers in the Status column of the Ministry Involvement–Community worksheet.
4) **Serving in the World:** Enter the total number of members and attendees who meet your established criteria for Ministry Involvement in the World. In the sample, the formula in F2 adds the numbers in the Status column of the Ministry Involvement–World worksheet.

> 5) **Total Involvement:** Enter the total number of members and attendees who meet your established criteria for Total Ministry Involvement. In the sample, the formula in H2 adds the numbers in cells B2, D2, and F2.
>
> 6) **Percentages:** To find the percentage in each category: Divide the total number serving in that category by the Total constituents (column A). The formulas in cells C2, E2, G2, and I2 perform these calculations for the sample. Keep in mind that the totals shown here do not account for duplications (i.e., persons who meet the involvement criteria in more than one category).

Chapter 6: Who Are Your New Leaders?

Measuring New Leader Development

Define "new leader" using the following criteria:
- A person currently in a leadership role who at the beginning of the evaluation period (usually one year ago) was not in a leadership role of any kind in your church.
- Be sure to distinguish between governing leaders and ministry leaders.

Define "leadership role" to include:
- In a ministry or program role (Small group, women's ministries, teacher, etc.)
- In a governance or management role (Board or committee member, church officer, etc.)

Establish and/or update your database of leaders at the beginning of the measurement period, identifying each existing leader by name, category of leader, and level of leadership.
- Categories
  - Ministry
  - Governance (Administrative)
- Levels
  - Level 1 Leader: Highly Capable Individual
  - Level 2 Leader: Contributing Team Member
  - Level 3 Leader: Competent Manager
  - Level 4 Leader: Effective Leader
  - Level 5 Leader: Executive Leader (Typically paid staff)
  - Total Number of Current Leaders

At the end of your measurement period update your database and count the number of names that did not appear on your previous list. That number constitutes the number of new leaders you have raised up for that year.

Instructions for Using the Leadership Development Worksheet:

1) Define "leader." Be sure to distinguish between governing leaders and ministry leaders.
2) When a potential leader is identified, enter his or her name in the spreadsheet.
3) **Recruited:** Enter the date the potential leader was recruited.
4) **Trained:** Enter the date that training (mentoring, shadowing, instruction, etc.) is completed, and the person is ready to assume leadership.
5) **Deployed:** Enter the date the newly trained leader begins his or her first leadership role.
6) **Levels:** If you choose to use levels to distinguish varying categories of leadership (those of Jim Collins from *Good to Great*, or your own) define each level and label the columns accordingly. If you choose to use levels, enter a 1 in the appropriate column when a person is deployed.
7) **Total:** At the end of each year, count the number of people deployed within a year. That total represents the number of new leaders your church raised up and deployed in that year. A simple formula for counting the number of names in a column for this purpose is "Counta" (see cell L1 for an example).

Chapter 7: Do You Really Grow by Staying Small?

Measuring Small Group Participation

In its simplest form and at the core, you are measuring the percentage of your constituents or attendees who participate in at least one small group. If you choose to measure by constituent rather than mere average worship attendance, you must define *constituent*. Typically constituents are those who consider the church as "their church," and participate with some regularity in the life of the church. The most obvious and easiest constituents to identify are your members. Regular attendees and even periodic attendees are constituents.

- Create a database listing each constituent (or attender) by name.
- Create a list of your church's small group opportunities. You may choose to categorize your small groups.
    - Bible Study, Discipleship, Spiritual Disciplines
    - Interest-based
    - Recovery
    - Evangelism
    - Mission or Ministry (Church-based, on campus)
    - Mission or Ministry (Community-based, primarily off campus)
- Calculate the percentage of your constituents (or attendees) who are involved in small groups.

Instructions for Using the Small Group Participation Worksheet:

1) Define "small group participation." Determine the level of engagement in a small group that constitutes full participation.
2) Enter the names of all members and attendees. If you are using the Ministry Involvement–Church worksheet, you can copy and paste the list of names from columns B and C of that worksheet.
3) As each member and attendee meets your criteria for small group participation, enter a 1 beside their name in the Participating in Small Group column.
4) To find the percentage of members and attendees participating in a small group: Add the numbers in the Participating in Small Group column and divide the sum by the total number of members and attendees. The formula in cell D1 performs this calculation for the sample. It will update as you enter data.

Chapter 8: What's More Important than Dollars?

Measuring Stewardship Effectiveness by Tithers

Both approaches to measuring stewardship training effectiveness require that you know how many households are represented in the church.

Establish a database, listing households by name. To measure the extent to which your church is a church of tithers:

- Create and implement a process that enables households to indicate whether or not they tithe. Provide a form asking for their name and a simple yes or no response to the question, "Does your household tithe (give 10 percent of your income) to the church?" Administer in a variety of ways allowing each household to respond in the most convenient way for them. Administering the survey might include:
  - A 3 x 5 card distributed, filled in, and returned at a church service
  - A 3 x 5 card distributed in Sunday school classes, Bible studies, and other church meetings
  - A link on the church's website that allows them to log on and respond
  - A mailing that includes a self-addressed, stamped return envelope with the form
- Based on the number of yes responses, establish your church's benchmark.
- Establish a goal to increase the percentage of households reporting that they tithe.
- Create and implement a plan to achieve your goal.
- One year later repeat the process described in the first bullet and compare the percentage of tithing households to the previous year's percentage.

To measure the extent to which your church is a tithing church:

- Discover the average annual household income for the communities included in your parish area.
- Divide that figure by ten to arrive at a tithe of the average income.
- Multiply the average household tithe by the number of actual households in your congregation. This figure represents an actual tithe for your church.
- Divide your church's contribution income for the year by the actual tithe amount calculated above. The result will be the percent of the composite church income actually given by your people.
- This figure is your church's benchmark.
- Establish a goal to increase the percentage of a tithe actually given by your church's households.
- Create and implement a plan to achieve your goal.
- One year later repeat the process described in the first four bullets of this section and compare the percentage given in the current year against the percentage given the year before.

Instructions for Using the Tithing–Self Identified Worksheet:

1) Enter the family name for all household units associated with your church in column A. A household unit may be any of the following: husband and wife, single head of household, single or multiple income. If the household has more than one adult, include first names of the adults in columns B and C.

2) Ask each household if the members of the household tithe (give at least 10 percent of their income) to the Lord's work. Each household will determine for itself the criteria for the answer. If the household says yes; enter an L in the column for the year you are tracking.

3) Ask each household if the members of the household tithe (give at least 10 percent of income) to the church. Each household will determine for itself the criteria for the answer. If the household says yes, enter a C in the column for the year you are tracking.

4) If a household answers yes to both questions, enter a B in the column for the year you are tracking.

5) Add the number of Ls + the number of Bs for the year to find the total number of households who report tithing to the Lord's work. The formula in cell E3 performs that calculation for the sample for the year 2007.

6) Add the number of Cs + the number of Bs for the year to find the total number of households who report tithing to the church. The formula in cell E5 performs that calculation for the sample for the year 2007.

7) Add the number of Bs to find the total number of households who report tithing to the Lord's work and to the church. The formula in cell E7 performs that calculation for the sample for the year 2007.

Instructions for Using the Tithing–Whole Church Worksheet:

1) Identify the communities you consider to be your church's "parish area" (i.e., the communities from which people could readily commute to your church for worship and other regular programs and activities).

2) Discover the average annual household income for the communities included in your parish area. Record that number in column B (see cell B2 of the sample row).

3) Add up the number of households in your congregation and enter that number in column C for the year you are measuring. If you are using the Tithing–Self Identified worksheet, the formula "=COUNTA('Tithing–Self Identified'!A:A)-1" will calculate that number for you.

4) Multiply the average household income for your parish area by the number of households in your congregation. This figure (see cell D2 in the sample row) represents the composite or projected income for the households in your church. In the sample row, the formula for this is "=B2*C2".

5) Enter the total contribution income for the year in column E (see cell E2 in the sample row). To find the percentage of income actually given by the households in your congregation: Divide your church's contribution income for the year (column E) by the projected income for the church's households (column D). The result will be the percentage of the church income actually given by your church's households (see cell F2 in the sample row; the formula is "=E2/D2"). This figure is your church's starting point.

6) Establish a goal to increase the percentage of a tithe actually given by your church's households. Record that goal on this worksheet (see sample in cell G1). Create and implement a plan to achieve your goal.

7) Repeat steps 1 through 5 at the end of each year and compare the percentage given with that of the previous year.

NOTES

1. The Fear of Numbers
1. SMART goals are Specific, Measurable, Aligned, Results-oriented, and Time-constrained.

2. If You Could Count Only One Thing
1. Find the *cost* by making two calculations, both of which start with the number of baptisms and/or confirmations. To arrive at the *cost* in people, take the average worship attendance for the year and divide it by the number of baptisms and/or confirmations. To arrive at the *cost* in dollars, take the total church income for the year and divide it by the number of baptisms and/or confirmations. See the Conversions worksheet on the spreadsheet you can download at www.abingdonpress.com/downloads.

3. How Many and How Often?
1. Ruckman, *Charles Finney, 1792-1875, Evangelist, Educator*, http://www.believersweb.net/view.cfm?ID=66, March 12, 2003.
2. Ruckman/Unknown, *Mordecai Ham, 1878-1959, Baptist Evangelist*, http://www.believersweb.net/view.cfm?ID=66, March 17, 2003.
3. See the Worship Attendance worksheet on the downloadable spreadsheet for a template that calculates average weekly worship attendance by year.
4. Dr. John N. Vaughan, *50 Most Influential Churches*: http://www.thechurchreport.com/mag_article.php?pageno=1&mid=671&pname=July&pyear=2006, Christy Media, LLC, July 2006.
5. In 2006 the California State Department of Finance reported the population of these cities as: Lake Forest=77,859; Rancho Santa

Margarita=49,130; Mission Viejo=97,997; Laguna Niguel=66,178; Laguna Woods=18,334; Laguna Hills=33,225, and Irvine=195,785 (http://www.dof.ca.gov/html/demograp/reportspapers/estimates/ rankings/citycounties1-06/documents/rankcities.xls).

6. See the Market Share worksheet on the downloadable spreadsheet for a template that illustrates these calculations.

7. See the Worship Frequency worksheet on the downloadable spreadsheet for a template that calculates the percentage of weeks per year each attendee or member attends worship.

4. How Many Stay?

1. Yogi Berra, *The Yogi Book: I Really Didn't Say Everything I Said!* (New York: The Workman Press, 1998), 36.

2. I find it interesting that Jesus apparently used the imagery of salt before light and the city on a hill. Perhaps He intended that penetration be primary and attraction a secondary strategy. If this is true, more churches are using the secondary strategy as their first or even only one. This could contribute to the lack of growth experience by so many churches today.

3. The bibliography contains numerous good books on this subject. Let me highlight two, *The Externally Focused Church* by Rick Rusaw and Eric Swanson and *The Shaping of Things to Come*, Michael Frost and Alan Hirsch.

4. *The American Heritage® Dictionary of the English Language*, Fourth Edition (Boston: Houghton Mifflin Company, 2004).

5. Commonly something like, "Those living in geographical proximity who could potentially become a part of our church."

6. See the Visitor Retention worksheet on the downloadable spreadsheet.

5. How Many Serve?

1. Alex Ayre, *The Wit and Wisdom of Mark Twain* (New York: HarperCollins, 2005), 24.

2. See the Ministry Involvement–Church worksheet on the downloadable spreadsheet.

3. Brennan Manning, *The Signature of Jesus* (Sisters, Oreg.: Multnomah Press, 1996), chapter 9, especially p. 191.

4. See the Ministry Involvement–Community worksheet on the downloadable spreadsheet.

5. See the Ministry Involvement World worksheet on the downloadable

spreadsheet. Also, see the Ministry Involvement Composite worksheet for a template that produces a summary of all levels of congregational Ministry Involvement (church, community, and world).

6. The apostle Paul made tents in order to enable his ministry in Corinth (Acts 18:1-3). We do well when we encourage people to follow in his footsteps.

7. I am grateful to Timothy M. Klinkenberg of St. John's Lutheran Church for permission to share the church's good practices with readers.

6 . Who Are Your New Leaders?

1. By *leadership community*, I mean: the senior pastor, associate pastors (if any), and lay leaders including both governance or board members and key ministry leaders.

2. Mary Kay Ash, *Miracles Happen* (New York: HarperCollins, 1994), 51. Erskine Bowles quotation from John F. Harris, "Chief of Staff Considers Governor's Race," Thursday, August 13, 1998; Page A1, http://www.washingtonpost.com.

3. Since the best place to identify leaders is in the leading, you will find a close tie between the idea of identifying leaders by helping them create a leadership track record in the subsequent section, "Train the Recruited."

4. Jim Collins, *Good to Great* (New York: HarperCollins, 2001), 20.

5. A *skill* is a natural or acquired ability to do a certain thing well. A leader may use his or her skill as a surfer or skier to create an outreach ministry to unchurched surfers or skiers. A *spiritual gift* is a God-given aptitude that is to be used for the good of the church. Spiritual gifts include such things as preaching, teaching, administration, and hospitality. Lists of spiritual gifts are found in Romans 12; 1 Corinthians 12; and 1 Peter 4 among other passages.

6. Parker Palmer, *Let Your Life Speak* (San Francisco: Jossey-Bass, 2000), 49.

7. Http://en.thinkexist.com/search/searchquotation.asp?search=leadership&page=1.

8. Russ Bredholt, interviewed by Patricia Baldwin, "The Strategist," *Private Clubs Magazine Online*, October 2005, http://www.private clubs.com/archives/2005-sept-oct/life_capital_ideas.htm.

9. An excellent resource for supervisors is *Execution: The Discipline of Getting Things Done* by Larry Bossidy, Ram Charan, and Charles Burck (New York: Crown Business, 2002). Of particular value are the questions

effective supervisors ask in their leadership role. These questions are not found in a list but are sprinkled throughout the book. They are well worth culling and collecting.

10. Among numerous good examples of churches that effectively raise up new leaders, my personal favorite is New Hope Christian Fellowship Oahu. New Hope's philosophy of "doing ministry as a team" is lived out in a highly effective way. New Hope is my choice for "Best Practice Church" in this area of ministry. I am grateful to New Hope Christian Fellowship Oahu for permission to use the church's name.

11. See the Leadership Development worksheet on the downloadable spreadsheet for a template that tracks the stages of leadership development discussed here.

7. *Do You Really Grow by Staying Small?*

1. Billy Graham founded The Billy Graham Association. Bill and Vonette Bright founded Campus Crusade for Christ. Louis Evans Jr. formed The Hollywood Christian Group. Jim Rayburn founded Young Life. Richard C. Halverson never founded an organization but provided leadership to many. Halverson was Associate Executive Director of International Christian Leadership, Washington, D.C., and was president of Concern Ministries, Inc. (charitable foundation). He was Chair of the Board of Directors, World Vision, Inc., a member of advisory boards of both the Navigators and the Orient Crusades Mission.

2. What follows is from notes taken at a meeting of pastors with Aaron Couch, one of Real Life's founding pastors. The meeting was held at Ross Point Camp, in Post Falls in September of 2006. I am grateful for their permission to share it here.

3. They have, for example, a China Hut, an Africa Hut, a Philippines Hut, and so forth.

4. I am grateful to National Community Church for permission to share the church's good practices with readers.

5. See the Small Group Participation worksheet on the downloadable spreadsheet.

8. *What's More Important than Dollars?*

1. This well-known and often-told story of Fred Craddock's is from his sermon "Who Cares?" available through http://www.preaching.com. The Shakespeare quotation is from *Hamlet*, act 5, scene 2.

2. There is a wealth of resources to assist pastors and other church lead-

ers develop people as tithers. Randy Alcorn's *Treasure Principles: Discovering the Secret of Joyful Giving* (Colorado Springs: Multnomah, 2005) is an excellent resource. Crown Ministries, Good Sense, and similar organizations have helpful materials. Another good resource is *Giving and Stewardship in an Effective Church: A Guide for Every Member*, by Kennon Callahan (San Francisco: Jossey-Bass, 1992).

3. If preachers were covering the whole counsel of God, they'd be addressing such things as reducing debt, paying bills on time, managing credit cards, living within one's means, and giving to the church. Brian Kluth of *Maximum Generosity* (http://www.kluth.org/) says in the introductory lecture of his seminar "Forty Days to a More Generous Life" that the Bible contains 30 verses on baptism, 225 on prayer, 300 on faith, and 700 on love, but at least 2,350 on money, finances, and material possessions.

4. A potential problem with this method is you tempt people to lie. Remember, people who seldom lie will often lie about tithing.

5. See the Tithe–Self Identified and Tithe–Whole Church worksheets on the downloadable spreadsheet.

6. Specific, Measurable, Aligned (with the mission and vision), Results-oriented, and Time-constrained.

7. Since my recommendation starts at 4 percent you can safely assume that I seldom find a church that is already giving at a 4 percent or more rate.

9. What Product Are You Producing Anyway?

1. While I recommend reading "all things Drucker," I think *Managing the Non-Profit Organization: Principles and Practices* (New York: Harper Collins, 1990) is his seminal and classic work for all church and ministry leaders.

2. I am grateful to Joe Boerman of Immanuel Church for permission to share the church's good practices with readers, including the qualities of the Spiritually Mature Disciple, which is framed and posted at the church as an ongoing reminder and inspiration.

SELECTED RESOURCES

Evangelism

Gladwell, Malcolm. *The Tipping Point: How Little Things Can Make a Big Difference*. New York: Little, Brown and Company, 2002.

Keller, Ed and Jon Berry. *The Influentials*. New York: The Free Press: A Division of Simon and Schuster, 2003.

Rosen, Emanuel. *The Anatomy of Buzz*. New York: Currency-Doubleday, 2002.

These three books are highly unlikely to be listed under "evangelism." Each deals from its own perspective with the subject of influencing people to change by word-of-mouth or relational "marketing." *The Tipping Point* reminds us that a few can cause the many to make certain choices. The book jacket of *The Influentials* states, "One American in ten tells the other nine how to vote, where to eat, and what to buy." *The Anatomy of Buzz* promotes the power of customer-to-customer selling. The concepts in these three books often have direct correlation to Christian witness and evangelism.

Lewis, Robert with Rob Wilkins. *The Church of Irresistible Influence*. Grand Rapids: Zondervan, 2001.

This is the transferable story of a church that has successfully "taken it to them" by building bridges to the community for the sake of the gospel.

Minatrea, Milfred. *Shaped by God's Heart: The Passion and Practices of Missional Churches*. San Francisco: Jossey-Bass, 2004.

Missional churches, among other things, mobilize their laity and take the gospel to the community. The theological foundations of *Shaped by God's Heart* and the stories of churches that live out their theology

121

enrich many of the theological and philosophical themes addressed in this book.

Poole, Gary. *Seeker Small Groups: Engaging Spiritual Seekers in Life-Changing Discussions*. Grand Rapids: Zondervan, 2003.
The book lays out a detailed step-by-step process for launching effective evangelistic small groups. The model is highly transferable, adaptable to a variety of evangelistic approaches and systems.

Rusaw, Rick and Eric Swanson. *The Externally Focused Church*. Loveland, Colo.: Group 2004.
Rusaw and Swanson offer a guide to mobilizing lay people in community-impacting ministry, made alive and accessible through telling the stories of churches that have done it.

Wilkins, Scott G. *Reach: A Team Approach to Evangelism and Assimilation*. Grand Rapids: Baker Books, 2005.
Evangelism should be natural and easy to do effectively. *Reach* promotes an approach to evangelism that is natural, non-threatening, and effective. By combining relational evangelism with a team mind-set, the *Reach* approach touches the unchurched and unbelieving where they are, guiding them to Christ and ultimately to involvement in the ministry of the church.

Retention, Assimilation

Lawless, Charles E., Jr. and Chuck Lawless. *Membership Matters: Insights from Effective Churches on New Member Classes and Assimilation*. Grand Rapids: Zondervan, 2005.
This book offers field-tested and proven suggestions for effective membership classes based on research gathered from churches across the United States. Its greatest strength is its emphasis on assimilation's *endgame*, ministry involvement.

Wilkins, Scott G. *Reach: A Team Approach to Evangelism and Assimilation*. Grand Rapids: Baker Books, 2005.
See comments above.

Lay Mobilization

Bossidy, Larry and Ram Charan. *Execution: The Discipline of Getting Things Done*. New York: Crown Business, 2002.

This book is an excellent resource for those who supervise others. Culling a list of the supervisory questions sprinkled throughout the book makes the read well worth the effort.

Bugbee, Bruce, Don Cousins, John Schmidt, and Willem A. Van Gemeren. *Network: The Right People in the Right Places for the Right Reasons.* Grand Rapids: Zondervan, 1994.

Network provides practical help in establishing a system of lay mobilization built on gifts, skills, passion, and call model. It also includes a helpful assessment instrument and training materials.

Bugbee, Bruce. *What You Do Best in the Body of Christ: Discover Your Spiritual Gifts, Personal Style and God-given Passion.* Grand Rapids: Zondervan, 2005.

This most recent manual for use in assessing people for ministry includes updated discussion questions and an assessment tool.

Leader Development

Borden, Paul D. *Direct Hit: Aiming Real Leaders at the Mission Field.* Nashville: Abingdon, 2006.

Direct Hit is a practical, succinct blueprint for pastors and lay leaders who wish to effect transformational change in their churches.

Foss, Michael W. *Power Surge: 6 Marks of Discipleship for a Changing Church.* Minneapolis: Fortress Press, 2000.

Written from the perspective of pastors and lay leaders, this book clearly lays out an approach to developing leaders from within. It introduces a systematic plan for developing leaders from within—from the crucible of ministry involvement through a "Young Leaders' Forum," all the way to pastoral leadership.

Jackson, John. *Pastorpreneur: Pastor and Entrepreneurs Answer the Call.* Friendswood, Texas: Baxter Press, 2003.

Jackson gives a strategic and systemic look at leading transformational change.

McNeal, Reggie. *A Work of Heart: Understanding How God Shapes Spiritual Leaders.* San Francisco: Jossey-Bass, 2000.

Using the lives of four biblical leaders, Reggie McNeal brings into focus the real-life ways by which God shapes leaders for His purposes. This Divine sculpting goes far beyond skills, personality traits, and even spiritual gifts. McNeal demonstrates how God shapes the hearts of leaders to reflect His heart.

Quinn, Robert E. *Deep Change: Discovering the Leader Within*. San Francisco: Jossey-Bass, 1996.
Deep Change is a classic on leadership in general and effective change-agentry in particular. This book is a must read for any pastor or lay leader who desires to lead for change.

Small Groups

Donahue, Bill. *Leading Life-Changing Small Groups*. Grand Rapids: Zondervan, 2002.
This comprehensive guide to establishing a small group system covers the gamut of issues from mission, vision, and values to establishing, leading, and developing new small group leaders.

Easum, Bill and John Atkinson. *Go Big with Small Groups: Eleven Steps to an Explosive Small Group Ministry*. Nashville: Abingdon, 2007.
This book is a practical, user-friendly guide for creating and maintaining a small group system.

Financial Stewardship

Alcorn, Randy. *The Treasure Principle: Unlocking the Secret of Joyful Giving*. Sisters, Oregon: Multnomah Press, 2005.
Alcorn offers concise, articulate instruction for how to live in light of the fact that everything belongs to God. This book is profoundly challenging.

Lane, Charles. *Ask, Thank, Tell: Improving Stewardship Ministry in Your Congregations*. Minneapolis: Augsburg Fortress, 2007.
This book contains sound teaching of biblical principles linked to thorough and practical guidance on establishing a system for helping people grow as Christian stewards.

Powell, Mark Allen. *Giving to God: The Bible's Good News About Living a Generous Life*. Grand Rapids: Eerdmans, 2005.
Powell teaches a holistic view of stewardship that puts the stewardship of money in the context of whole of life stewardship.

Three helpful Web resources on financial stewardship are:
- Crown Financial Ministries: http://www.crown.org/
- Generous Giving: http://www.generousgiving.org/
- Willow Creek Good Sense: http://willowcreek.org/goodsense.asp

Growing Healthy Churches' Seedlings

Serving congregations who are committed to and accountable for their role in fulfilling the Great Commission

www.growinghealthychurches.org

...through reproducing Churches, Disciples, Leaders

Home

Who is GHC?

Dr. Borden's Seedlings

GHC Network's Articles

Upcoming Events

Online Store

Missions

Church Resources

Pastors Resources

Church Listings

Classifieds

Contact Us

Links

eNewsletter Sign Up

Give Online

GHCNetwork.org

Search

[ ] Go

Advanced Search

Growing Healthy Churches through serving congregations who are committed to and accountable for their role in fulfilling the Great Commission.

Our mission is growing healthy churches by networking, resourcing and encouraging churches in the areas of growth, health, transformation and church planting.

Our standard is excellence. We work with passion and with integrity. We're together.

Upcoming Events
2007 Annual Celebration
Guest Speakers: John & Trina Jenkins pastors from First Baptist Church of Glenarden in Landover, MD **Hosted by:** Community Baptist Church San Mateo, CA – *San Mateo Marriott* **October 11-12, 2007**
May 1, 2007, 08:01

Dr. Borden's Seedlings
Called to Serve the Living God
Apostolic people are those who are convinced that Jesus Christ is the bedrock foundation of everything that is important in this life ... they have produced the perseverance and faith described by both James and Peter in their letters to Christians. Jesus Christ is crucial ...
Jun 1, 2007, 16:30

GHC Network's Articles
Stages of Reproduction
Part of what we're about in the GHC Network is helping churches partner with and parent new churches. Some churches are excited about the possibilities and are on board with reproducing. Others seem disinterested in church planting. Still others find themselves in the middle of those options.
Jun 1, 2007, 16:29

Latest Headlines

Who is GHC?
New to GHC - Craig Fuller
Who is GHC & What is its Mission?

Dr. Borden's Seedlings
Called to Serve the Living God
Lives that Reflect God
Staying Focused

GHC Network's Articles
Stages of Reproduction
Beware of the Glitz
Managing the Madness

Upcoming Events
2007 Annual Celebration
Saddleback Church Worship Conference & Festival
Purpose Driven Youth Ministry - Student Leadership Conference

Online Store
Books, CDs, DVDs & eTeaching eCollege

Missions
Mission Giving
Summaries

GHC: A TEACHING NETWORK

Made in the USA
Lexington, KY
13 September 2016